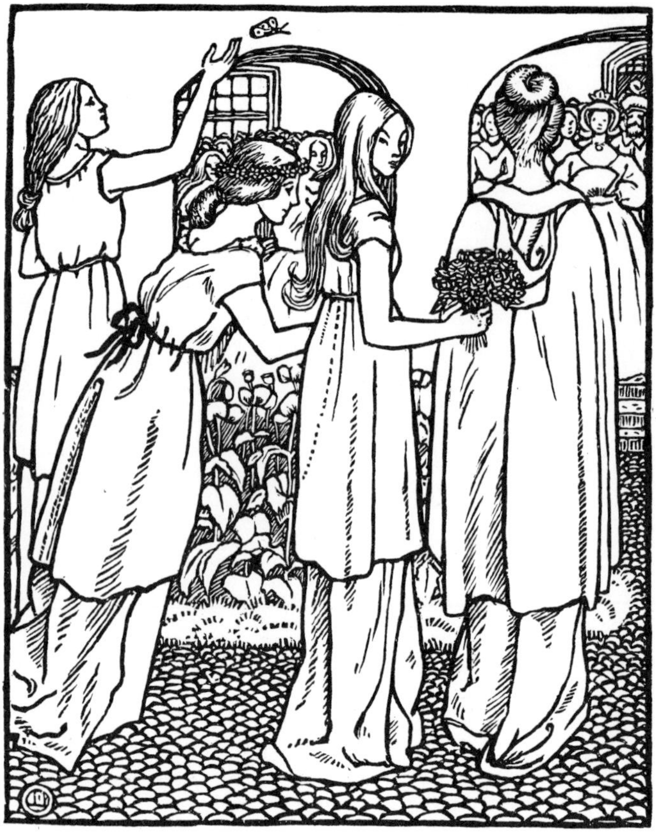

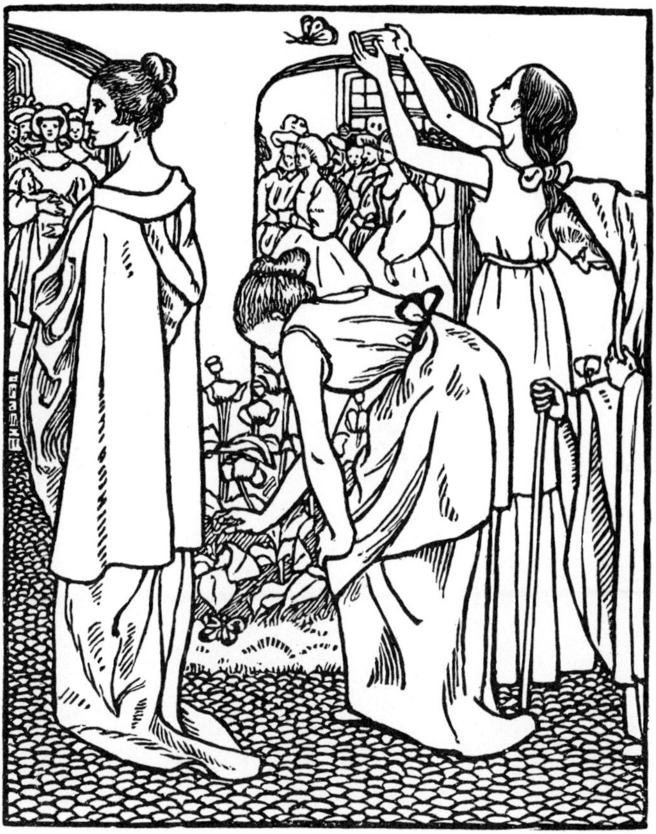

THE WOOD ENGRAVINGS OF LUCIEN PISSARRO & A BIBLIOGRAPHICAL LIST OF ERAGNY BOOKS

BY LORA URBANELLI

SILENT BOOKS AND THE ASHMOLEAN MUSEUM

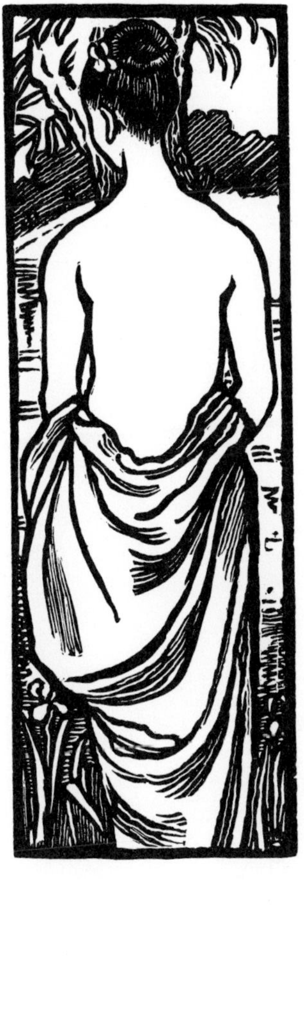

First published in Great Britain in 1994
by Silent Books, Swavesey, Cambridge, CB4 5QG
and The Ashmolean Museum, Oxford, OX1 2PH

Colour plate section funded by the Paul Mellon Centre for Studies in British Art.
The bookplates are reproduced from originals in The Butler Collection.

ISBN 1 85183 056 1 (Silent Books)

ISBN 1 8555 050 0 (Ashmolean Museum)

British Library Cataloguing-in-Publication Data.
A catalogue record for this book is available
from the British Library.

Typeset by Eye 2 Eye, Over, Cambridge

Printed in Great Britain by
Lavenham Press, Lavenham, Suffolk

All illustrations are reproduced same size unless indicated.

Front end papers Perrault *Deux Contes de ma Mère Loque,* (1899)
Title page Baigneuse (1900)
Title Verso Women in Roundel (1908)

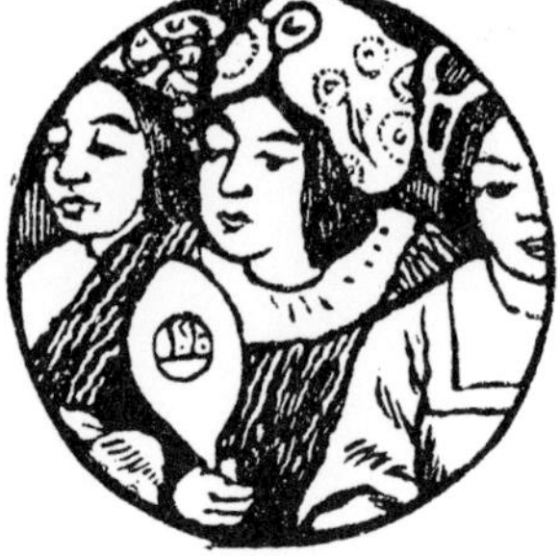

CONTENTS

LUCIEN PISSARRO, first son of the Impressionist artist Camille Pissarro, was a gentle man, shy and very quiet. Despite these attributes, and the clamorous orbit of the circle of artists around his father, Lucien grew to find his own voice. Under Camille's very loving, but somewhat overbearing watchful eye, he found his place, not among the great painters of Paris, but in England during a private press revival, which he not only helped to shape, but to which he made serious and unique contributions with his Eragny Press. Indeed, Lucien brought together, in a way that no one else at the time was able, the avant-garde ideas of the Parisian Neo-Impressionists and the rich tradition of English Arts and Crafts publishing embodied in the work and life of William Morris. The resulting synthesis, so graphically evident in the evolution of Lucien's wood engraving style, was completely his own.

Born in Paris on February 20th 1863, Lucien spent his first twenty years moving with the family, a group consisting of both parents, one surviving sister and four brothers[1]. As his father and the Impressionist painters struggled for recognition, the Pissarro family's financial burdens grew.

[1] In the following biographical sketch, as well as for general inspiration, I am indebted to Alan Fern and his unpublished dissertation "The Wood Engravings of Lucien Pissarro with a Catalogue Raisonné." I would also like to acknowledge the work of Marcella Genz, whose recent doctoral thesis in Library Science, "A History of the Eragny Press 1894-1914," includes a very useful clarification of biographical facts and an excellent analysis of the business records of the press.

Moving intermittently from Paris to Pontoise, Louveciennes, Britanny, London (during the Franco-Prussian War) and back to Osny, Camille rarely sold a painting in these years, and when he did he was forced to compromise on its price. The tenacious painter was a man of extraordinary artistic principle, however, and greatly respected by his colleagues. Moreover, he was a doting and devoted father and, though failing at the business of art, an admirable role model for the growing Lucien.

Notwithstanding the disapproval of Madame Pissarro, who would have preferred that her children, especially her eldest, learn a more lucrative and practical trade, Camille encouraged Lucien to focus his attention on art, to relentlessly study and draw from nature and to cultivate his painting skills. They frequently went on painting trips together, a practice that continued all their lives. Not surprisingly, Lucien's artistic approach derived from the elder Pissarro's and from a young age he painted in the Impressionist manner.[2] Later both men explored the scientific precision of Pointillism, conceived by their young friend Georges Seurat and the other Neo-Impressionists. Lucien, in a modest act of independence, remained true to the Pointillist technique throughout his life, despite his father's eventual dismissal and derision of it.

Lucien inherited more than a keen eye from his father. His lack of concrete business skills and, indeed, his disinterest in acquiring them, was evident from Lucien's

[2] For a complete catalogue raisonné of Lucien Pissarro's paintings, see Thorold, *Catalogue of the Oil Paintings of Lucien Pissarro*. The catalogue raisonné of the artist's prints is in the final stages of completion by the author and Alan Fern.

first job in 1878 at age fifteen and did not substantially improve with maturity. In 1883, nearly five years later, Lucien was sent to London to live with his uncle Phineas Isaacson; his parents, especially his mother, anticipated that he would overcome his shyness, improve his English, secure permanent employment, and perhaps augment the family income. While the first two objectives may have been met, the latter two were certainly not. He was, however, exposed to some great masters and, despite his mother's attempts to steer him otherwise and his father's weak efforts to concur, Lucien seems to have made the decision at this time to dedicate his life to artistic rather than business pursuits. Perhaps the most important realization of this trip, however, was the beginning of a lifelong rich and revealing correspondence between father and son.[3]

Osny, March 15, 1883

My Dear Lucien,
You do indeed show strength of will in harnessing yourself to English, nothing but English,...and your future, too, who knows? - do not give up drawing, draw often, always from nature, and whenever possible consult the primitives. - If you could only be persuaded that no other activity is so intelligent and agreeable. What would be perfect would be for you to become quite mad about art; Sundays and holidays would then

[3] See Rewald, *Camille Pissarro: Letters to his Son Lucien*, 1943; and the recently published Thorold, *Letters of Lucien to Camille Pissarro*, 1883-1903, 1993 (hereafter referred to as *Letters*). Also, Bailly-Herzberg, *Correspondance de Camille Pissarro*, in five volumes.

> become days of real happiness - you would await them with impatience,....[4]

As this brief passage indicates, Camille's message was a mixed one: enslave yourself to your senses, but, oh yes, try to reserve it for the weekends!

During his year abroad, the young Pissarro was surrounded by the people and the ideas that would shape his future as he toyed with concepts that he would later develop. He travelled with his cousin Esther Isaacson, his future sister-in-law, and discussed their mutual interest in Socialism. Through the Isaacson family he met his future wife, thirteen year old Esther Bensusan. He worked without pay for a music publisher, and studied diligently in the galleries of the British and South Kensington Museums. Lucien's letters home included enthusiastic descriptions of the great marbles, Chinese porcelains and Holbein drawings which he examined there.[5] He actively exchanged his own drawings with Camille, who in return sent Daumier prints to inspire him and special papers on which to work. One such paper was for "gillotage", a photomechanical means of reproducing drawings for journal illustrations. Although Camille disapproved of the popular process, it is

[4] Rewald, *Letters*, p. 24.

[5] *"J'ai vu à South Kensington des meubles extraordinaires. Il y a entre autre chose un meuble renfermant un panneau lequel est fait de petits morceaux de bois de differentes couleurs et plaequés représentant des figures, on pourrait faire des sujets modernes dan ce genre, ce serait vraiment revolutionnaire. Il y a aussi des porcelaines de Chine magnifiques, je me demande comment ils font pour avoir des tons aussi puissant."* As Thorold points out, Lucien would later be inspired by figures such as these found on Asian pottery and fashion them into wood engraved illustrations for Nerval's *Histoire de la Reine du Matin*, 1909, and Gautier's *Le Livre de Jade*, 1911. Thorold, *Letters*, pp. 31-33.

clear that both men were giving thoughts to ways for Lucien to combine art and commerce.

At home that summer, Paul Gauguin visited and painted with Camille. They discussed the concept of producing Impressionist inspired tapestries, pottery and fans as a way of disseminating their own art to a wider audience. At this time, a revolution in the industrial arts, one which considered everyday objects in terms of satisfying design and careful craftsmanship, was already underway in England, thanks primarily to William Morris, and repercussions were beginning to be felt abroad. Lucien's letters from this period, however, made no mention of this movement which eventually was to have such a lasting effect on him. After a brief visit home, during which he went on painting excursions with his father, Lucien finished out his year in England, and finally returned to France in March of 1884 to help the growing family settle into their new house in Eragny sur Epte.

The following six years for Lucien, until his permanent relocation to England, were vital to his artistic development. During this period he divided his time between Paris and Eragny. While in the country he painted with his father, experimented with etching and, inspired by his discovery of the work of Kate Greenaway and Walter Crane, designed and illustrated children's stories for his younger siblings. In Paris Lucien obtained a job with the firm Manzi for which he worked making plates for colour printing,[6] and studied the proper art of wood engraving

[6] As quoted in Fern, p. 22, Lucien felt that the instruction gained at Manzi was essential to his later mastery of printing wood engravings in colour.

 with August Lepère. To his great credit, Lepère was careful to emphasize the non-commercial aspects of the medium to his young student, despite his own reputation for slick presentation.

In the wood engraving 'Le Curé', from 1885[7] (Figure ii), Lucien shows his early concern for reproducing the exact appearance of his drawing on the wood. In essence denying the strictures of the medium, he cut the image to the contours of his pen line, and created an effect more like a woodcut (removing wood around the line) than a wood engraving (incising the block to create a white line). This approach to the block would change dramatically over the next decade.

In 1885 Lucien and Camille began to associate with Georges Seurat, Paul Signac and Félix Fénéon, whose interests ranged from social anarchism to the development of new theories in colour perception which would later be termed Pointillism and Neo-Impressionism.[8] With support from his father and these new friends, Lucien began to seek out a means to publish his drawings, whether in the form of a children's book or as illustrations in any of a multitude of contemporary French publications. In the

[7] The work is signed "L. Vellay", Madame Pissarro's maiden name. He used this alias for a short time at Camille's advice, in order not to be associated with his father, who felt his work to be too unpopular with the buying public. According to the notebook in the Pissarro family archives at Ashmolean Museum's, this work was published in *La Vie Moderne*, 1 October 1887.

[8] As noted earlier, both Camille and Lucien began to paint at this time in the Pointillist technique. Camille abandoned the method in 1890, finding it too restrictive. Lucien, when he painted, continued throughout his life to apply pointillist principles.

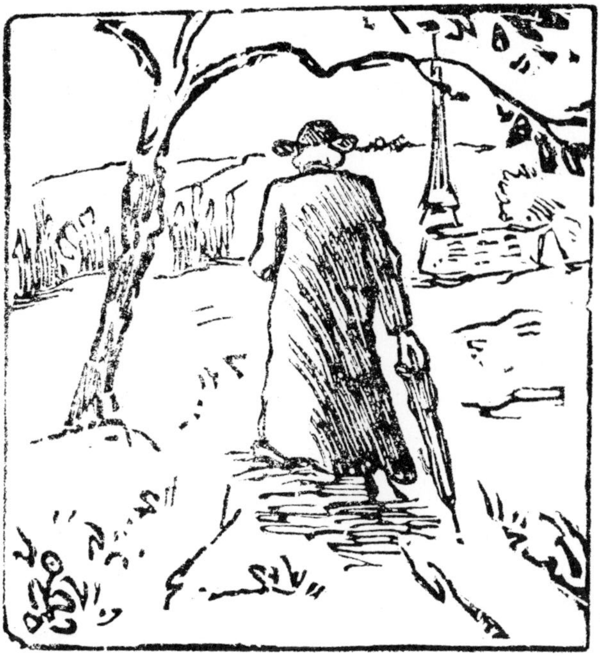

Figure i *Le Curé* (c. 1884)

former quest he was frustrated, in the latter, he enjoyed mixed success. The most important commission for Lucien at this time was the illustration of Octave Mirbeau's "Les Infortunes de Mait'Liziard" published in *La Revue illustrée*, 15 June 1886. Although well received among friends, the work was considered too unpolished by the reading public, accustomed to a more refined presentation. (Figure ii) Lucien's drawings and wood engravings appeared intermittently over the years in *Le Chat noir*, *La Vie Moderne* and, starting in 1890, in the anarchist journal *Père Peinard*.

In the meantime, quite independently of his father, the younger Pissarro's stature as an artist was beginning to grow. He began to exhibit paintings, drawings and prints on a regular basis in, among others, the eighth and final Impressionist exhibition (1886), the second exhibition of the *Société des Artistes Indépendents* (1886), with *Les XX* in Belgium (1887) and in *Les Peintres-Graveurs* at Durand-Ruel (1889). His work, especially his wood engravings, was well reviewed.

By the end of the decade, Lucien had become more engrossed in making prints. Indeed, it was only in the medium of printmaking that he finally acquired an independence of style and expertise although from the time that he began learning to print, Lucien worked at the task of reproducing his father's drawings. Both men spoke often of collaboration, especially as Lucien's knowledge of colour printing became more sophisticated. Their first joint project was not to see fruition until 1893,[9] but Lucien's body of work began to reflect this mutual desire, despite his inability to find financial backing. Moreover, his love of children's book illustration was finding no custom in Paris. Both father and son began to realize that perhaps the only way for Lucien to take advantage of his developing skills and to reach his aspirations was to live

[9] *Les Travaux Des Champs*, published by The Vale in 1893, consisted of six wood engravings by Lucien after drawings by Camille. Three were single colour, three were printed with up to six blocks of colour. See below p. 24. Lucien did not complete the larger, more complex collaborative project that he wanted to in Camille's lifetime. '*La Charrue d'Erable*', perhaps Lucien's tour de force, was not published until 1912. See below, p. 40.

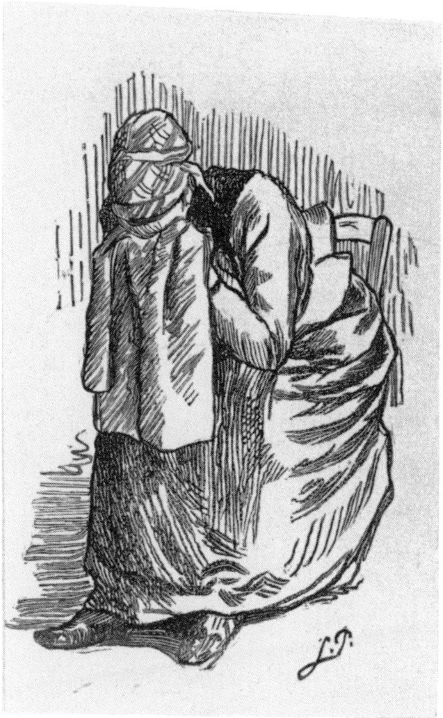

Figure ii Mirbeau *Les Infortunes de Mait' Lizziard* (1886)

and work in a more congenial atmosphere. The position which England held in support of the decorative arts was well known. The Pissarros were also convinced that the English public was more receptive to the graphic arts. After a visit to London in the Spring of 1890 with his father and the artist Maximilien Luce, it became clear that if Lucien wanted an independent career in his new found *métier* he would have to leave France. That November Lucien moved to England permanently.

Within a few months of his arrival Lucien began to move in the circles of those artists who were shaping the private press movement. If one were to date the onset of this movement, it would have to be two years earlier with a lecture given at the first Arts and Crafts Society Exhibition in London (18 November 1888). Entitled "Letterpress Printing and Illustration", it was delivered by Emery Walker, a friend and neighbour of William Morris, and relied heavily on Morris's own collection of 15th century illuminated manuscripts for its lantern slides. Already a noted proponent of the aesthetic re-evaluation of shoddy, mass produced household goods, Morris also championed reform of the social and industrial systems which had alienated craftsmen from their product in the first place. His devotion to what became the Arts and Crafts revival motivated him to set up his legendary crafts workshop. By the time of Walker's lecture, Morris had also been experimenting with book design through the Chiswick Press, a commercial operation, as a means of publishing his own writings. After the speech, Morris approached Walker about his desire to design a new typeface to better suit his ideas, "to re-attain a long-lost standard of craftsmanship of book printing".[10] In 1890, inspired by the large lantern slide projections of coloured borders and beautiful type, Morris succeeded in establishing his own press operation with his own typeface designs, which brought the craftsman, the artist and the printer together under one roof, the Kelmscott Press.

[10] Roderick Cave, *The Private Press*, p. 104.

William Morris looked to Gothic design for inspiration when creating his books. The overall aesthetic product was heavy with decoration. He used special papers specifically designed to emulate 15th century Bolognese papers, had gold specially hammered for his gold leaf and encouraged British binders to produce a proper vellum for his covers. Although beautiful as objects of art, they were criticized by some as "overdressed", as books that asked to be looked at and admired, but not read.[11] The Kelmscott Press, however, was very successful commercially. Although only in operation for seven years, it became a large, profitable organization, ironically almost commercial in its production. In that short span the press produced 52 books in 66 volumes. Illustrations were provided by the artist Edward Burne-Jones and, although woodcuts and wood engravings were used in the production, they were all carved by a technician after Burne-Jones' drawings. Morris himself never printed at his own presses, but instead masterfully directed a substantial staff of others. William Morris died in October of 1896, but not before witnessing the great outpouring of interest in the book-beautiful that Kelmscott books had generated, both at home and abroad. Close associates Sydney Cockerell and Emery Walker carried on for eighteen months to finish out editions, but sadly, much was abandoned.

Just as Kelmscott Press was being established, Lucien Pissarro arrived on the scene. Thanks to a letter of introduction to the poet John Gray written by his friend Fénéon, Lucien was brought into the circle around Charles

[11] Ibid., p. 111.

 Ricketts and Charles Shannon, two young artists who hosted salon style gatherings at their studio in Chelsea named "The Vale".[12] These gatherings entertained the likes of Laurence Housman, Oscar Wilde, George Bernard Shaw, William Butler Yeats, Roger Fry and the painter William Rothenstein, among others. As a group of artists and writers their interests were varied, but they enjoyed engaging in the polemic of reconciling John Ruskin's theories with more modern aesthetic concerns.[13] In this regard their interest in avant-garde art was very welcome to Lucien; in turn, they gladly received Lucien's introduction to French Symbolist literature. The Vale group was also interested in wood engraving as an art form and, in addition, was hungry for contact with other contemporary (read "continental") artists.

Ricketts founded the Vale Press soon after Kelmscott was underway and was unavoidably influenced by Morris' undertaking. Rather than look to Gothic design, however, he was more interested in the simpler early Renaissance books of Aldus Manutius.[14] Wishing to avoid what he characterized in Kelmscott borders as designs "full of wine", Ricketts proclaimed that, Vale's books were to be "full of light."[15] In contrast to Morris' dense border vegetation, Ricketts' designs were cleaner and, as a result, his books more approachable. Vale books were printed at the

[12] The Vale had previously belonged to Whistler.

[13] Fern, p. 39.

[14] A facsimile edition of Manutius' *Hypnerotomachia Poliphili* from 1499 had just been released in England in 1888. Darracott, *World of Charles Ricketts*, p.37.

[15] Ibid., pp. 48-49.

Ballantyne Press and, like Morris, Ricketts chose not to be presumably involved in that process. However, he was responsible for the first progressive step away from Morris by insisting that artists cut their own wood engravings for illustrations.

At long last Lucien's love of book making and illustration was to find fruition at the Vale through Ricketts' interest not only in making his own contribution to the private press movement, but also in publishing the work of other artists. 'Twelve Woodcuts in Black and Colours by Lucien Pissarro', frequently referred to as the 'First Portfolio', was published by the Vale in 1891, though not completed and distributed until 1893. It included three multiblock colour pieces for which Lucien was beginning to establish quite a reputation. The five-colour print 'Le Fagot' (Figure iii), actually begun in 1889 while Lucien was still in France, was shown to the Morris circle by Emery Walker. Lucien reported to Camille that they were very impressed with his abilities in colour wood engraving, the likes of which they had never seen.[16]

Lucien was invited to contribute to Ricketts' occasional publication, *The Dial*, and did so in 1892 with his wood engraving, 'Sister of the Wood' (Figure iv). Of this work Camille exclaimed: "méfie-toi des préraphaélites".[17] It is true that stylistically the Vale group had an immediate impact on Lucien, and his work did begin to show the influence of the Pre-Raphaelite artists Burne-Jones and Dante Gabriele Rossetti. But not having been trained in the

[16] Thorold, *Letters*, p. 169.

[17] "Beware the Pre-Raphaelites!" Ibid., p. 200.

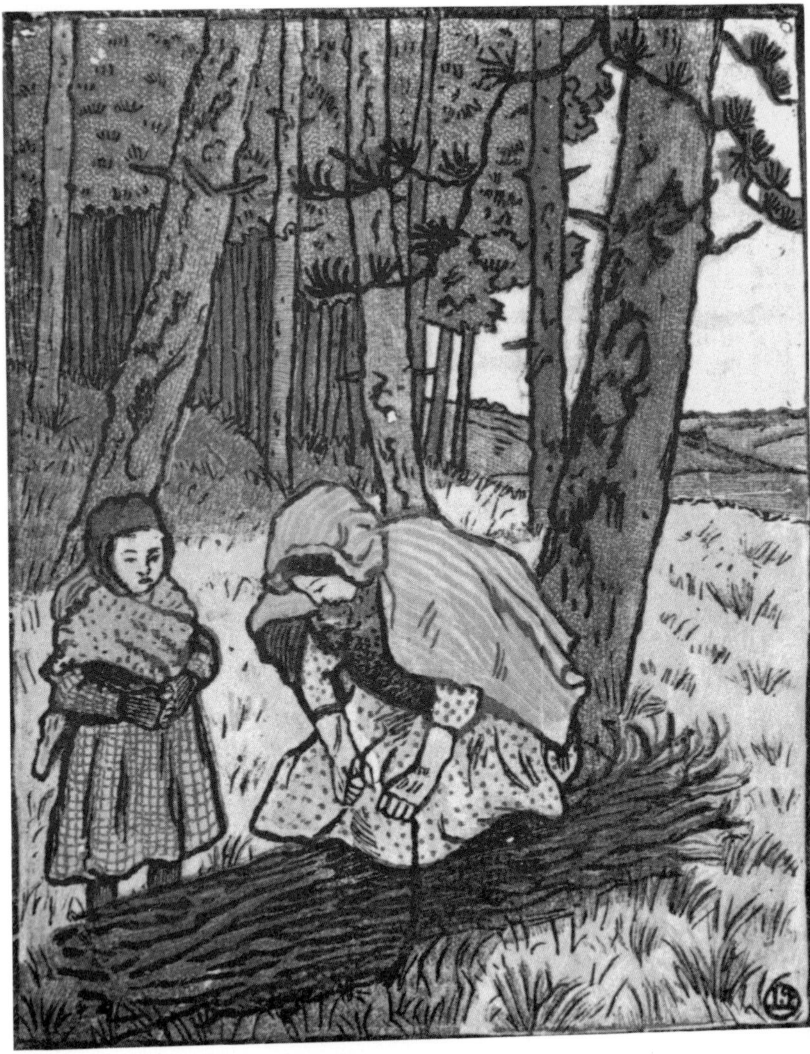

Figure iii *Le Fagot* (1889) reduced

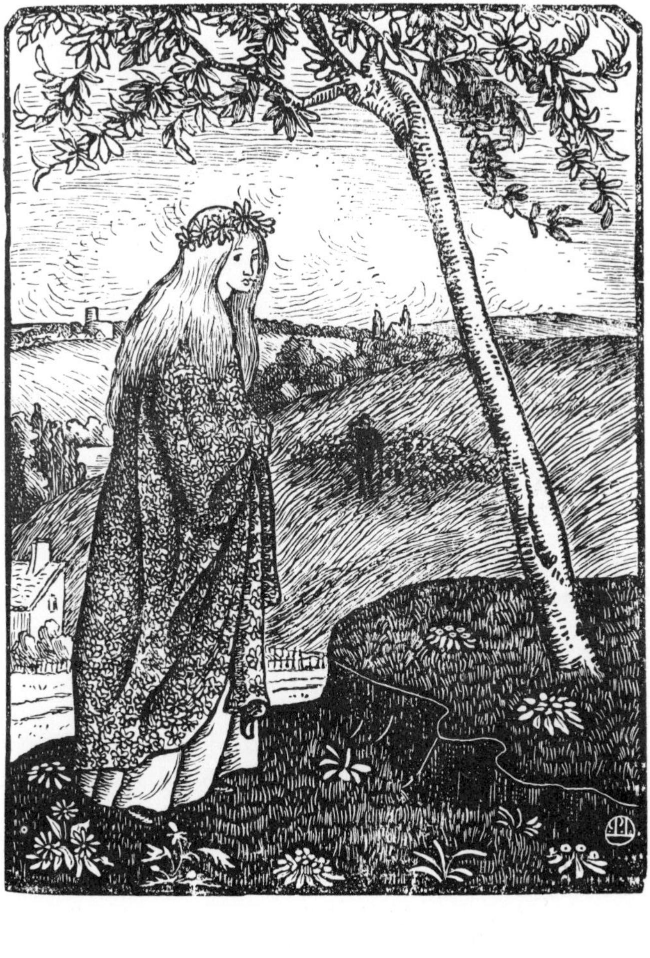

Figure iv *Sister of the wood* (1891) reduced

English academic tradition, Lucien's work maintained a French character and a slightly naive quality, which his father urged him to preserve and nurture.

The following year a selection of Lucien's and Camille's collaborative prints was published by the Vale in a small portfolio of six images. Entitled 'Les Travaux des Champs', and editioned in 25 copies the work was not a commercial success. That is not to say that the joint effort was futile. Particularly satisfying was the work, 'Femmes Faisant de l'Herbe', a six-colour block print showing each artist at his graphic best. (Figure v)

Despite Camille's growing disquiet with his son's new friends, Lucien's association with Ricketts and Shannon gave him focus and provided him with career choices which were nothing like his father's. His stylistic explorations allowed him to begin to define himself and afforded him occasion to argue for that self-definition against Camille's better judgment. Equally as important for Lucien were the business opportunities that his Vale affiliation generated when he began to publish his own books.

In early 1894 Lucien wrote to Camille that he was busy at work cutting the blocks for a little book. He complained that the cost might prevent him from carrying the project through and, since it was something he had been working toward for so long, he hoped that perhaps Camille could afford to buy him a small press.[18] By now Lucien and his

[18] Ibid., p. 345. "*...Tu sais depuis combien de temps j'ambitionnai de faire un petit livre! A propos, je voudrai bien avoir une petite presse à main pour pouvoir faire le tirage moimême et assez vite – si je trouve quelquechose de pas cher* (of course) *est-ce que tu pourrais me donner l'argent pour l'acheter?*"

Figure v *Femmes Faisant de l'Herbe* (1893)

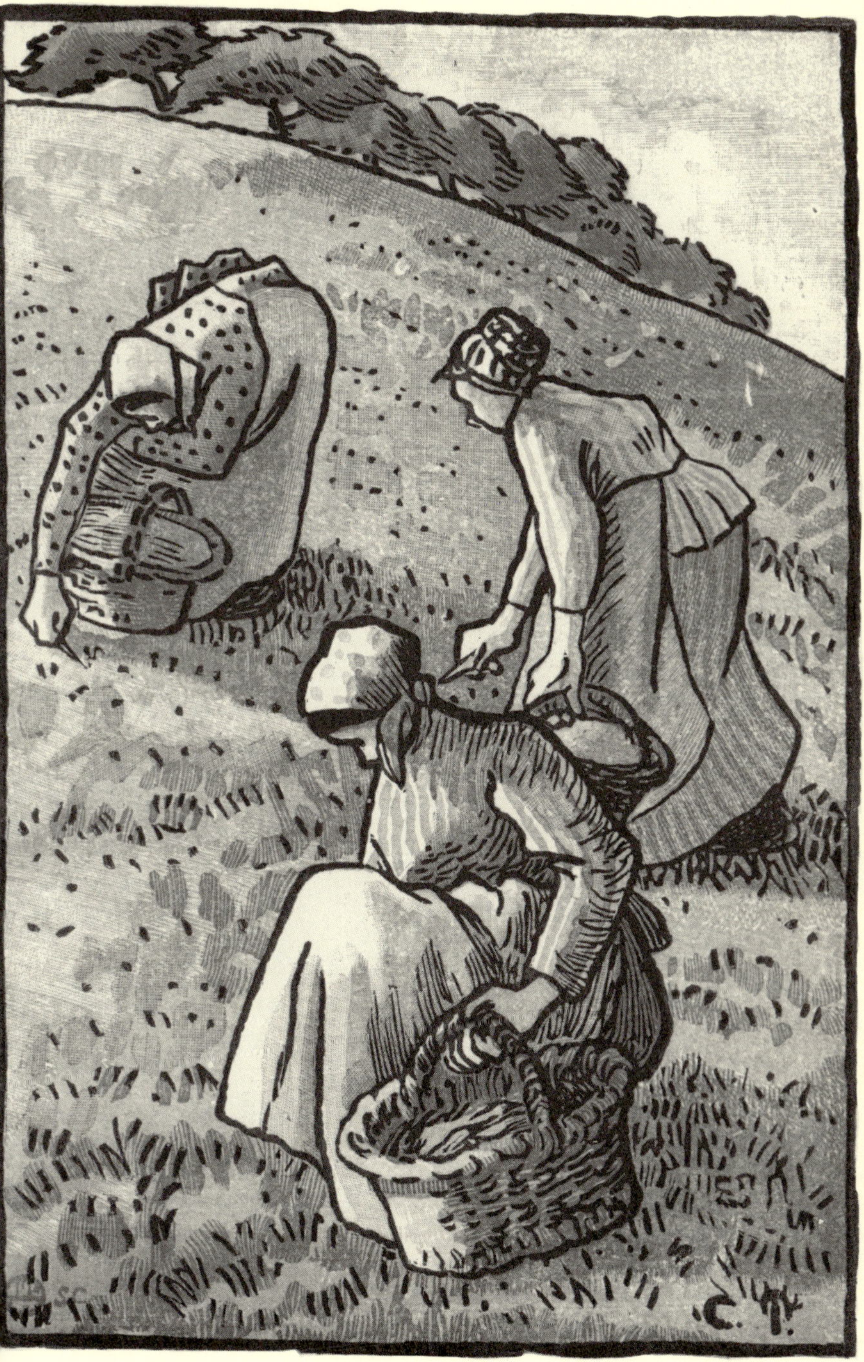

wife, Esther Bensusan Pissarro, and their new daughter, Orovida, were living just outside London in Epping (Essex) at the "Brook". With new equipment and space to set up a workshop, the Brook was the perfect place for Lucien and Esther to establish the Eragny Press, which they named after the Pissarro family's home village in France. Fortunately for Lucien, the Vale's new partner, Llewellyn Hacon, agreed to handle the business end of Lucien's future production. For a percentage of sales, Hacon and Ricketts supplied ink and paper for the Eragny Press and paid any extra printing costs.[19] Eragny books were then distributed through the Vale and marketed by John Lane at the Bodley Head; it was a happy arrangement for as long as it lasted.

That same year Lucien and Esther produced their first book with an Eragny Press imprint, *The Queen of the Fishes*. The story was an old Valois fairy tale which Lucien had been working on, in numerous versions, for many years. This final English interpretation, translated by Esther's friend Margaret Rust, was richly illustrated with colour prints and borders and lettered with photo-engraved calligraphy for the text, which was printed in grey ink. (Figure vi) Lucien's involvement in every step of this intricate procedure allowed him to indulge in a true joining of letter forms and illustration, a dimension of design that would concern him for his entire career.

Queen of the Fishes was well received. As a first book it was rather experimental, and yet it maintained that *naiveté* and

[19] This and other details of the business arrangement between Lucien and Hacon & Ricketts are detailed in Genz, p. 95.

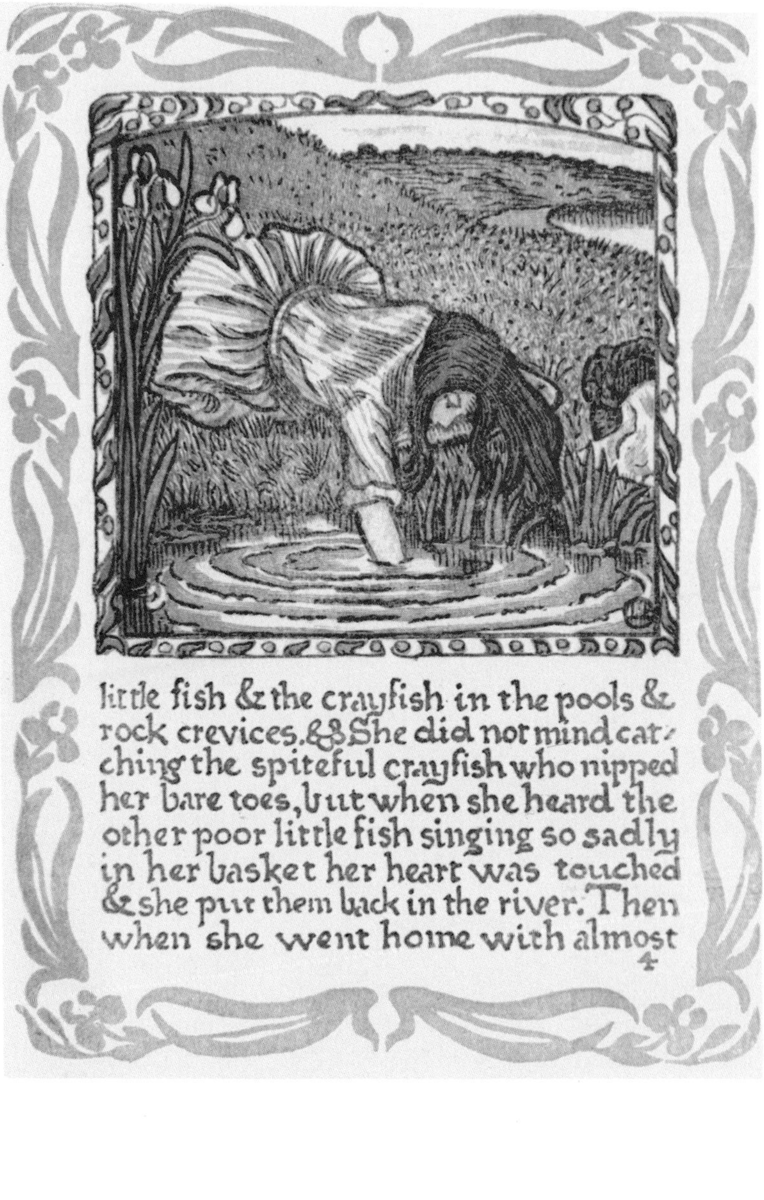

little fish & the crayfish in the pools & rock crevices. && She did not mind catching the spiteful crayfish who nipped her bare toes, but when she heard the other poor little fish singing so sadly in her basket her heart was touched & she put them back in the river. Then when she went home with almost

4

Figure vi Girl reaching into a stream from *Queen of the Fishes* (1894)

freshness of character that had so defined the young Lucien. Sigfried Bing, director of *Maison de l'Art Nouveau*, exhibited the work at his *l'Exposition Inter-nationale du Livre Moderne* of 1896. Ambroise Vollard, who went on to become an important publisher of artists' books himself, said that at first he was disheartened by seeing this beautiful piece and wondered how anyone could top its perfection; but in the end, its beauty influenced his decision to go forward.[20]

Over the next nine years the Eragny Press continued its business arrangement with Hacon & Ricketts, who bought half of every edition outright and actually sold out one book before it came back from the binder.[21] This proved to be the most lucrative period of the press' twenty-year production, but in the end the operation was still not greatly profitable. Camille helped to finance the Press as much as he could until his death in 1903, but the younger Pissarros were always short of funds. Lucien, it seems, had learned a good but arduous lesson from his father: that artistic issues should always take priority over monetary concerns. Consequently, because of their high standards and production costs Lucien and Esther rarely made a profit.

The Eragny Press was truly a labour of love. Whereas Morris and Ricketts never actually printed at their presses,

[20] Ambroise Vollard, *Recollections of a Picture Dealer*, p. 170. When Vollard did begin publishing, he asked Lucien to illustrate with wood engravings Paul Verlaine's *Parallèlement*. Camille, however, advised his son to turn down the offer, claiming that Vollard was far too demanding and did not pay enough. The book was eventually illustrated by Bonnard with lithographs. Una Johnson, *Ambroise Vollard*, p. 24.

[21] That book was Perrault's *Deux Contes...*

Lucien and Esther designed the books, engraved all the blocks, set the type and blocks together, then painstakingly proofed and editioned all their work, occasionally hiring a printer to assist. Production was slow and their spoilage rate was high, especially when producing their later colour work. However, it was precisely their immense involvement that made their books, above any other, the only "genuine Arts and Crafts product".[22] Their commitment was absolute and their methods meticulous and almost entirely self-taught.

Despite using photography to transfer his drawings to the block, Lucien's engravings developed on the wood as he cut them. Sometimes, the more decorative blocks were cut by Esther after Lucien's drawings, or they occasionally shared that task. Esther, an artist in her own right, was a strong and opinionated woman and very much a presence in every aspect of the business. Aside from assistance in carving, she helped with the proofing and the running of the presses. Esther may have even been responsible for the trademark flower-patterned paper covers of Eragny books, as she was also known as an excellent gardener who tended the enormous garden at the Brook. Her talents, proved indispensable when, in 1897, Lucien suffered a stroke. It was two years before Lucien's health was finally restored, but the fingers on his left hand remained paralyzed. During this long recovery, Esther kept the press and the business active.

After *Queen of the Fishes*, the Eragny Press produced fifteen more books through the Vale. Thanks to Ricketts' generos-

[22] Genz, p. 53.

 ity, the books were set in the newly cast Vale type and sometimes even used Vale watermarked papers. In contrast to their first book, this next group of works contained little colour. These books usually contained a complex frontispiece with an illustration, a border and decorative capitals. Aside from ornamental fleuron at the end of lines and sections, the rest of the book was often left unadorned. The vigorous black and white patterning of these designs was reminiscent of Kelmscott and Vale books and reflected the height of England's influence on Lucien. Ironically, it was also in this distinctly Pre-Raphaelite period that many of the Eragny Press books were printed in French to attract continental collectors. (See Figures vii - x) Overall, early sales were moderately successful.

In 1903 everything changed. In that year Camille Pissarro, Lucien's guiding light and lifelong confidant, died at age 73. As if that were not enough, the Vale Press closed its doors after a damaging printer's fire and never re-opened. In one year the Eragny Press lost its two primary sources of financial and moral support. Luckily, the year before, Lucien had finally finished the designs for his own typeface and Camille had subsidized the production of the matrices and punches. He called it the "Brook" type and his last sixteen books were published using it. Brook type was a lighter, more subtle version of Vale, on which it was based, and perfectly suited to Lucien's Franco-English sensibilities. Colin Franklin has argued that "...Brook type, on the white paper of the small pages in Eragny books, was the most beautiful fount invented in this whole period."[23]

[23] Franklin, *Private Presses*, 1969. p. 98.

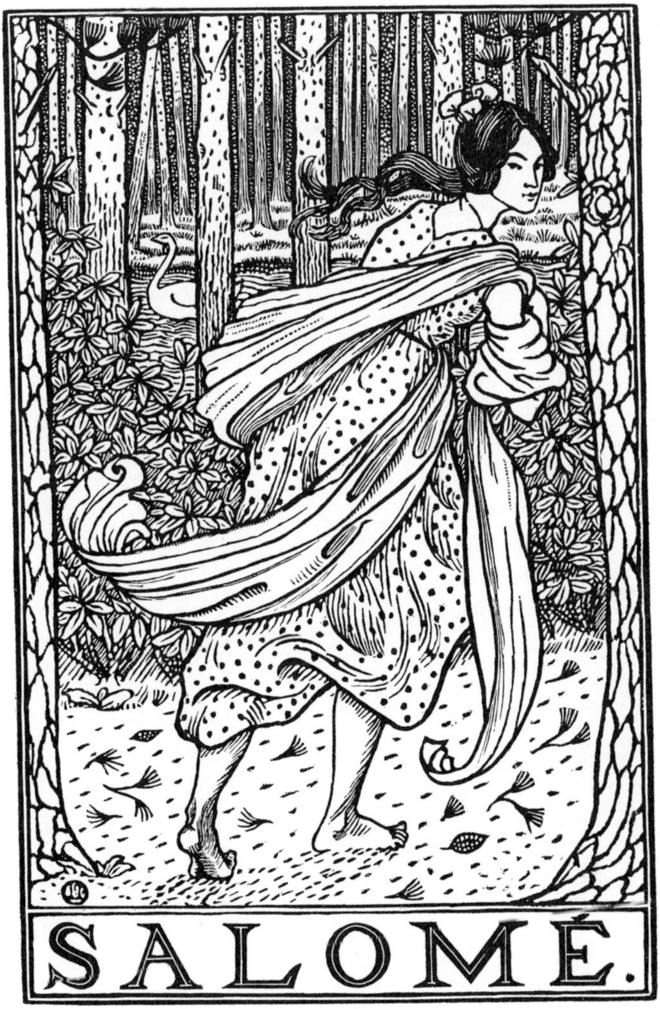

Figure vii Laforgue *Les Moralités Légendaire* I (1897)

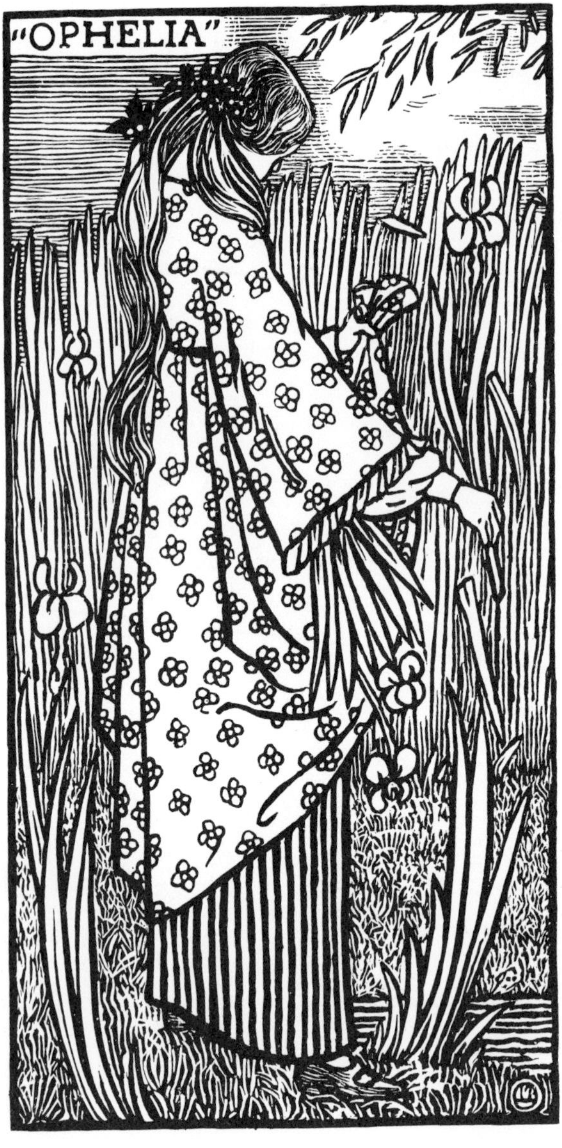

Figure viii Laforgue *Les Moralités Légendaires II* (1898)

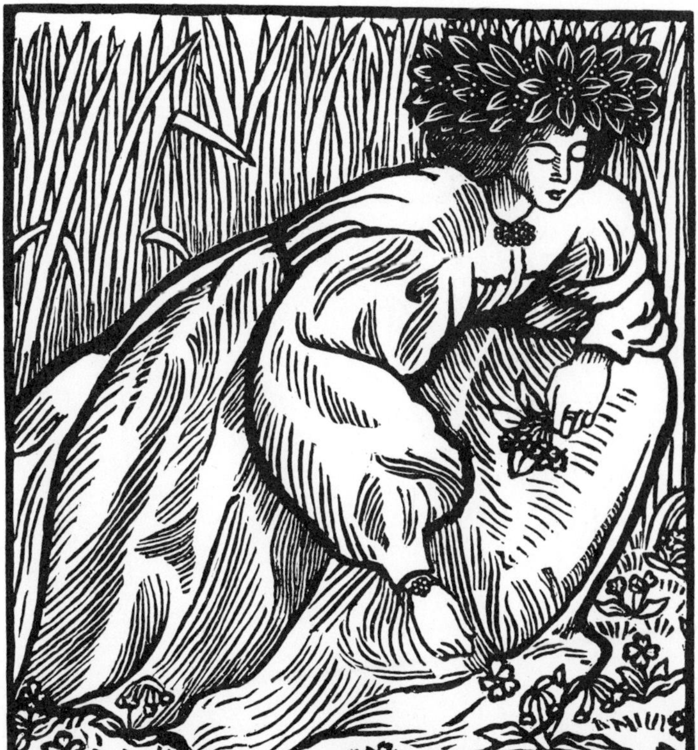

Figure ix Ronsard *Choix de Sonnets* (1902)

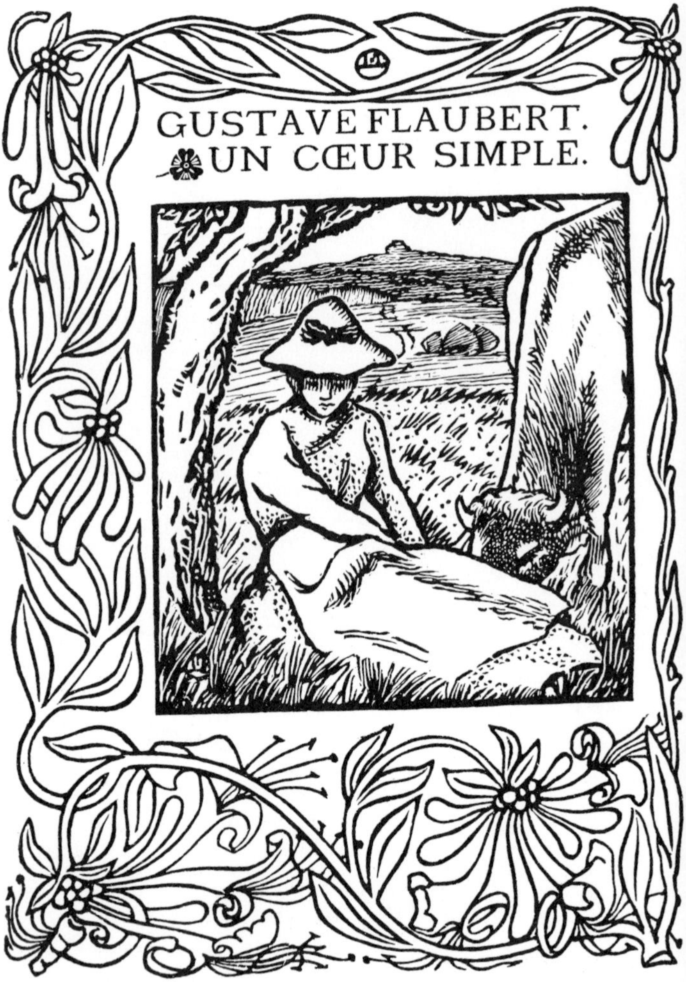

Figure x Flaubert *Un Coeur Simple* (1901)

Despite the setbacks of 1903, the last eleven years of production saw the return of colour to Eragny Press publications. In this work Lucien truly flourished. His renewed palette (opposing hues of red and green, yellow and purple) revealed his background in Neo-Impressionist colour theory, but his distinctive accomplishment was due in part to subtle inking. (see colour plates) Lucien almost never printed a colour flat. Each block, cut to print a single colour, was mottled to produce a pattern and inked with a delicate tint. The blocks of pale colour were then carefully printed one over the next so that the viewer had to look closely to understand what was causing the spectral vibration. The colours were printed wet on wet, and the paper was kept damp so that the sheet did not shrink between colour applications. Occasionally, Lucien even published an entire volume on coloured papers. *Abrégé de l'Art Poetique Français* by Pierre de Ronsard, 1903, has been seen printed on a light pink sheet, on light green, and occasionally with tinted inks, in addition to the regular black and white edition. Unfortunately, the re-introduction of colour meant an even larger outlay of time and money.

By 1905 Lucien and Esther had begun to reduce the size of their editions and the number of books produced in order to lower their costs. Whereas in 1903, at the height of their output, they published five titles in editions of around 240, in 1905 and again in 1906, they published only three, in editions of 200 or less. The following seven years, between 1907 and 1914 when the press closed, production dropped significantly and only a total of five books were produced in editions no larger than 130.

 Moreover, two of those books were wholly subsidized by publishing commissions.

In 1909 and again in 1912 the Eragny Press received the prestigious honour of requisitions to produce books from two French Bibliophile clubs. Each should have been a profit-making venture, but once again, due to highly technical production and Lucien's miscalculation of his expenses, any gains they might have made were wiped out. Gérard de Nerval's *Histoire de la Reine du Matin et de Soliman Ben Daoud* was commissioned by the Société des Cent Bibliophiles in 1909. The luxury of working with advanced capital and high quality materials enabled Lucien to construct a lavish book. Printed in colours and with gold leaf, it was excruciatingly detailed and took twenty months to produce.[24] The final composition included more than fifteen illustrations, seven border designs, and eleven historiated capitals. The leather-bound cover was patterned with gold-stamped flowers. (Figures xiii-xiv [see also colour plates])

Even more elaborate, though less ornate, was the book contracted for *Le Livre Contemporain* in 1911, *La Charrue d'Erable*. Finally, Lucien was able to interest a publisher in what had been his dream of a major collaboration between himself and his father. Ironically, the work may have been even better for the wait; for, after long negotiations with the

[24] Genz, pp. 189+. Lucien proudly used gold leaf in his work, not powder. The gold was always applied first so as not to stick to the wet ink of the other colors being used. First, the block was inked with a varnish and that varnish was printed on the damp paper. A gold sheet was then adhered carefully to the paper and hopefully stuck only to the varnished sections.

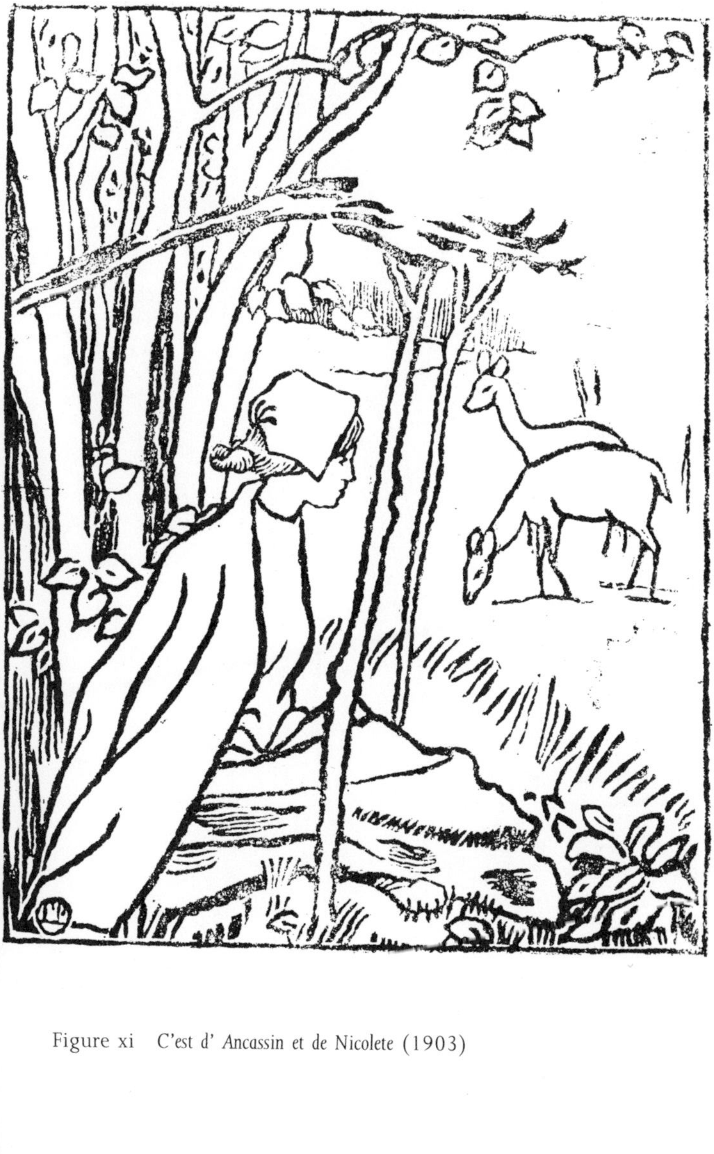

Figure xi C'est d' *Ancassin et de Nicolete* (1903)

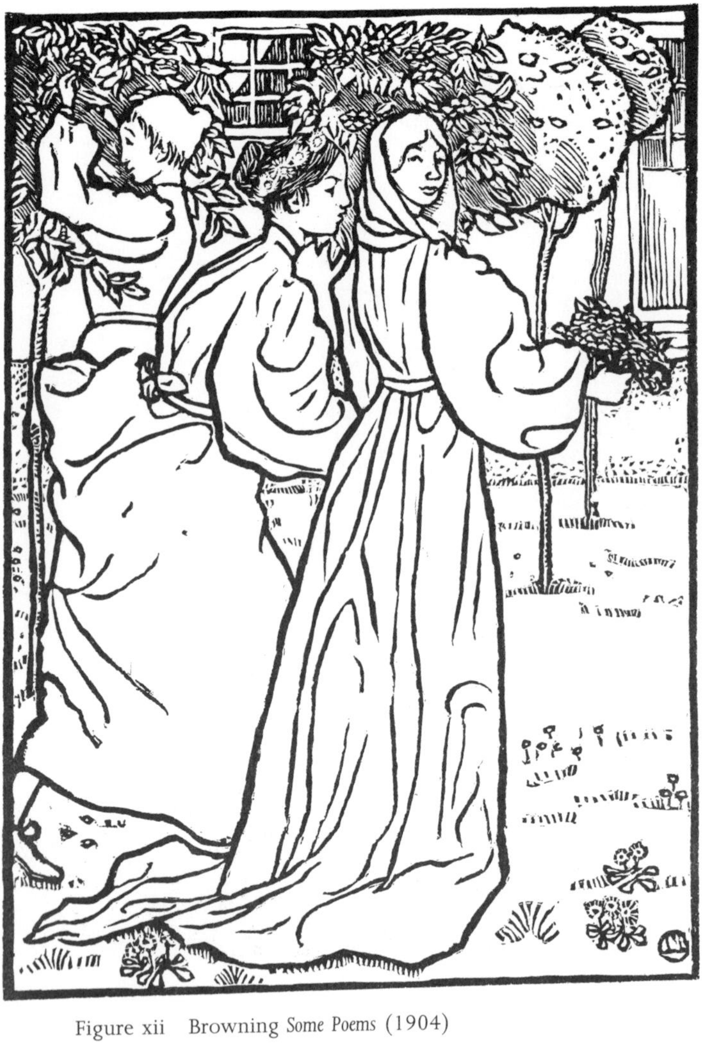

Figure xii Browning *Some Poems* (1904)

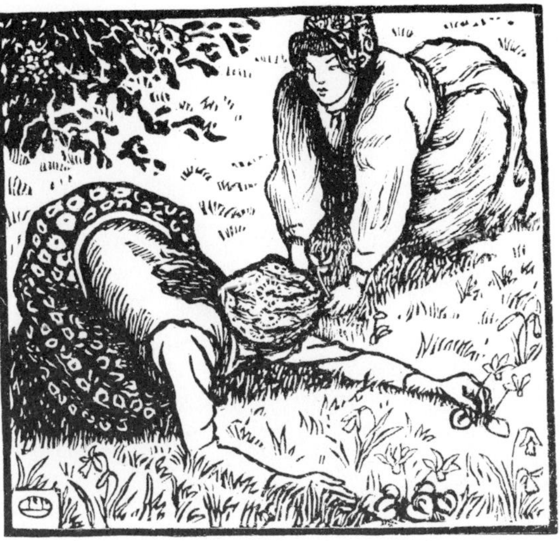

Figure xiii Nerval. Histoire de la Reine du Matin et de Soliman Ben Daoud (1909)

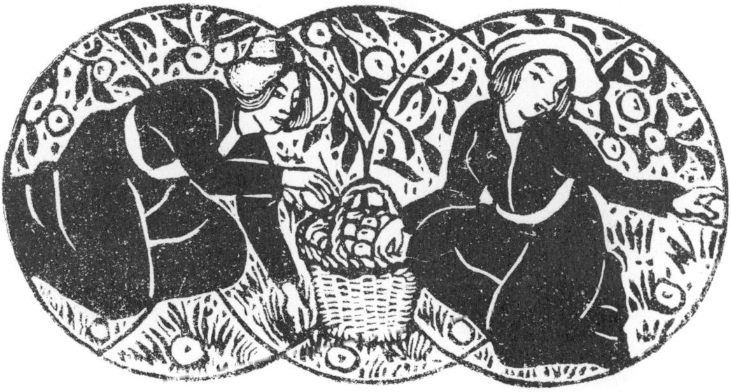

Figure xiv Nerval. Histoire de la Reine du Matin et de Soliman Ben Daoud (1909)

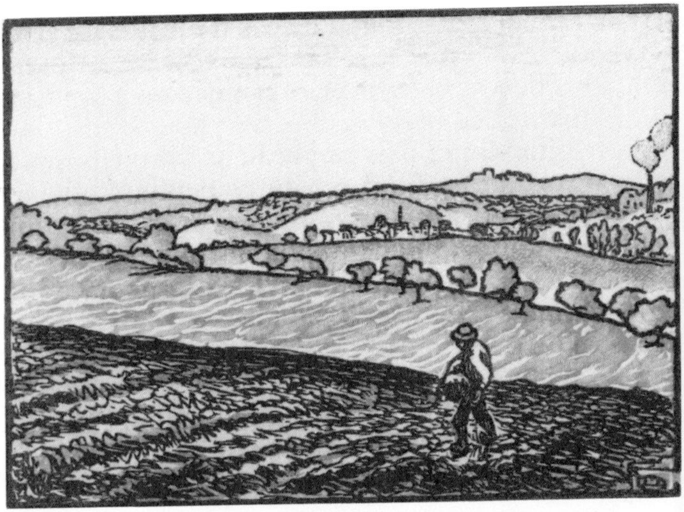

LES SEMAILLES.

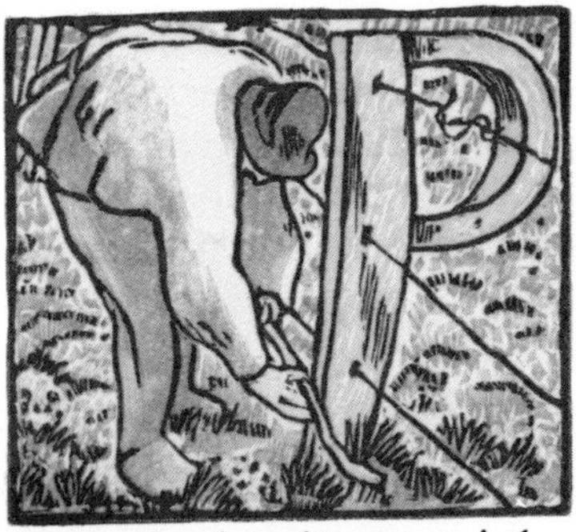

IERRE HERNEQUIN se tint, quelques instants, sur le seuil de sa maison, où tombait une averse tremblante de lumière.

Il avait enterré sa femme le matin même.

Le repas, qui suit ordinairement les funérailles, venait de prendre fin, et la dernière carriole, reconduisant les parents dans les villages éloignés, disparaissait au loin, tache mouvante qui se rapetissait, se fondait dans l'immensité brune de cette terre de Beauce.

27

Figure xv Moselly *La Charrue d'Erable* (1912)

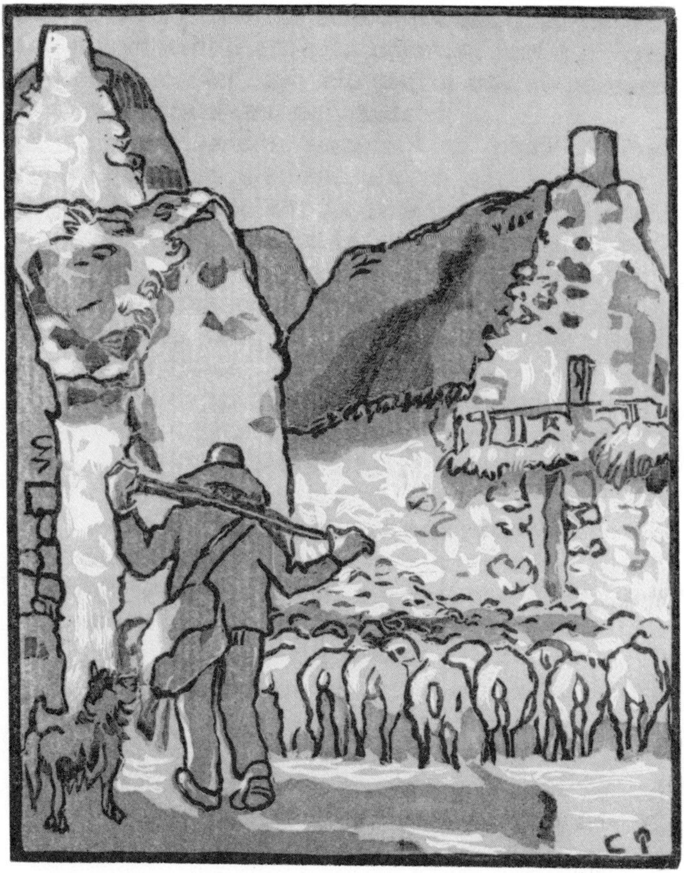

Figure xvi   Moselly *La Charrue d'Erable* (1912)

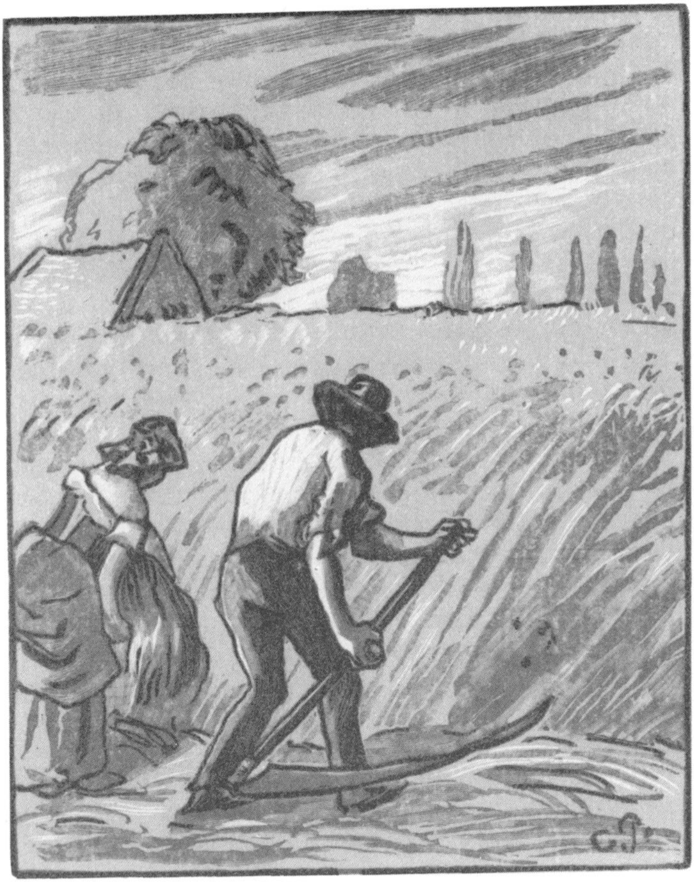

Figure xvii   Moselly *La Charrue d'Erable* (1912)

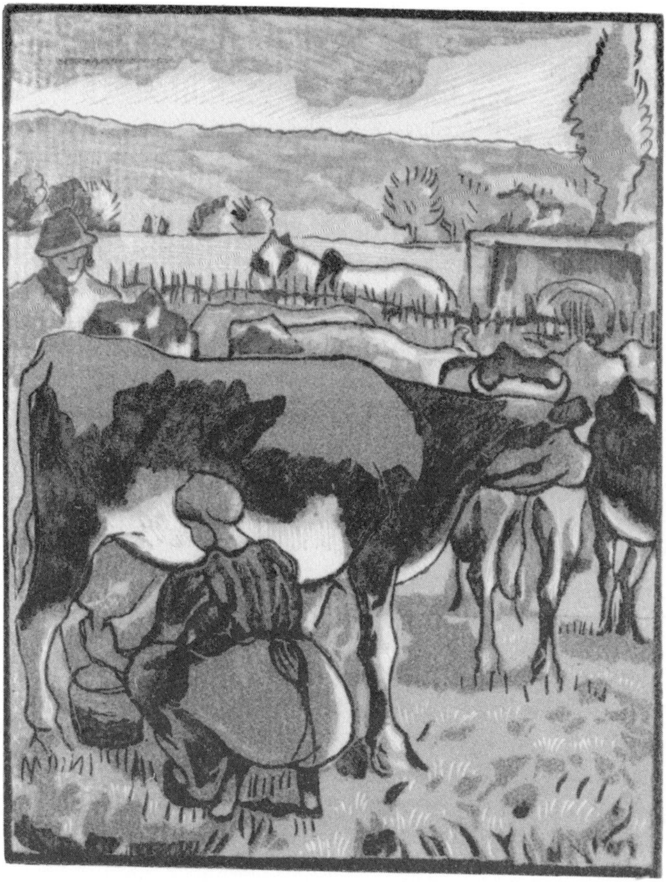

Figure xviii Moselly *La Charrue d'Erable* (1912)

publisher, not only did Lucien agree to produce the twelve woodcuts after his father's drawings, but he filled out the volume with many of his own creations. Each of Camille's twelve drawings, reproduced in the close tonalities of the chiaroscuro method, had a small chapter written around it by the writer Emile Moselly. Lucien then embellished the text with illustrated head and tail pieces and historiated capitals. The edition took more than two years to assemble and most of Lucien's profit was spent in production. (Figures xv-xviii)

When World War I broke out, the Eragny Press was forced to close. Lucien and Esther were no longer able to import their specially handmade paper from France, but more importantly, the War caused them to lose touch with their regular collectors not only on the continent, but worldwide.[25] Neither partner anticipated more than just a temporary halt to production, but when the war was over, they found themselves without the capital to begin again. Lucien, who had already returned to painting before the close of the Press, continued to paint and exhibit his work until the end of his life in 1944.

In its twenty years of operation the Eragny Press produced thirty-two titles. Included in those books were more than 300 wood-engraved illustrations, borders and fancy capitals representing about 70% of Lucien's entire printed oeuvre.[26] Unlike Kelmscott and the Vale before it, and the

[25] There were several serious collectors of Eragny Press books in the United States, including J.M. Andreini, H. Alfred Fowler and John Quinn.

[26] Lucien also made several lithographs and approximately thirty-four etchings.

many other private presses that began in the 1890s, the Eragny Press was not a lucrative business operation. The small format books were not highly priced yet were very labour intensive. Nor did they resemble their competitors in character. Eragny books, with their beautiful flowered covers, were unique in their skillful combination of French and English aesthetics. It was an unlikely synthesis of English Arts and Crafts design and French impressionistic interest in colour, light and sensations after nature. Ironically, this same charming quality may have made the work less marketable. Although Lucien chose his titles to appeal to a cross section of interests, to the English the books may have seemed too French, and to the French the books were a bit too English. Moreover, the volumes produced during the Vale association were printed in French to attract the continental collectors, but their aesthetic quality at that time was at its most Pre-Raphaelite. The second half of the Eragny output was almost all printed in English, yet they were perhaps the most "French" in character.

Ultimately, what made Eragny Press books extraordinary — their complex production methods combined with simple artistic integrity — resulted in small output, little-to-no profit, and eventually led to the demise of the Press. In 1947, three years after Lucien's death, Esther, with the help of her nephew, cast the punches and matrices of the Brook type into the English Channel. It was a symbolic gesture to the two countries whose influence had mingled so beautifully in Lucien's work and whose national characters had helped to define the output of this small, but important, private press.

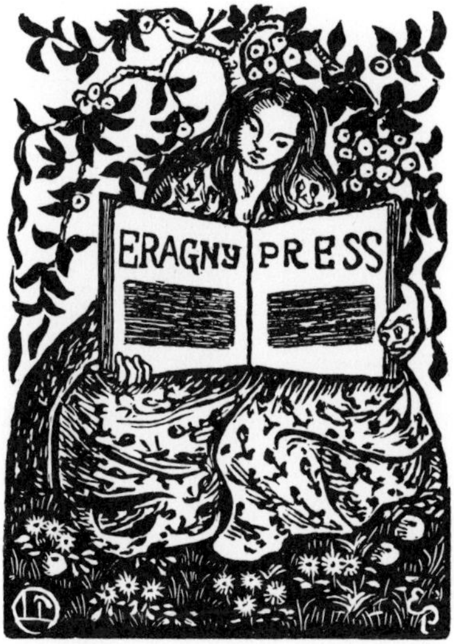

1. Press Mark I (1894)

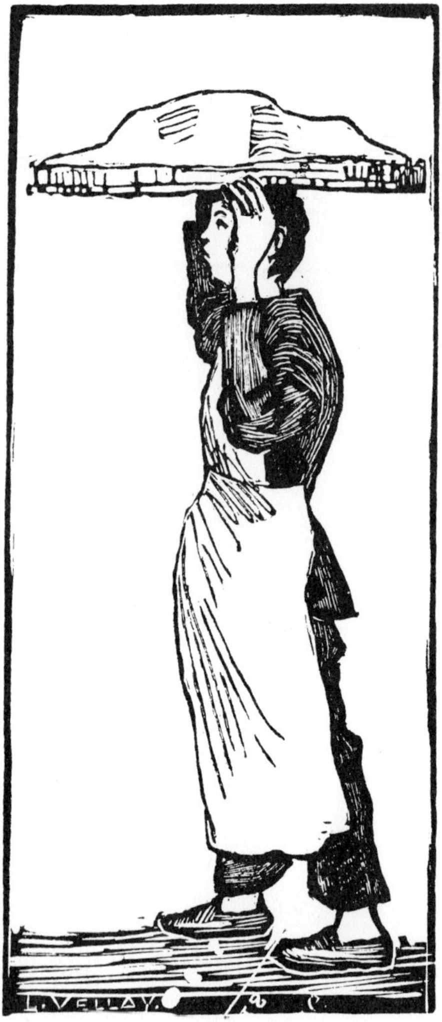

2. Le Pâtissier (c.1884)

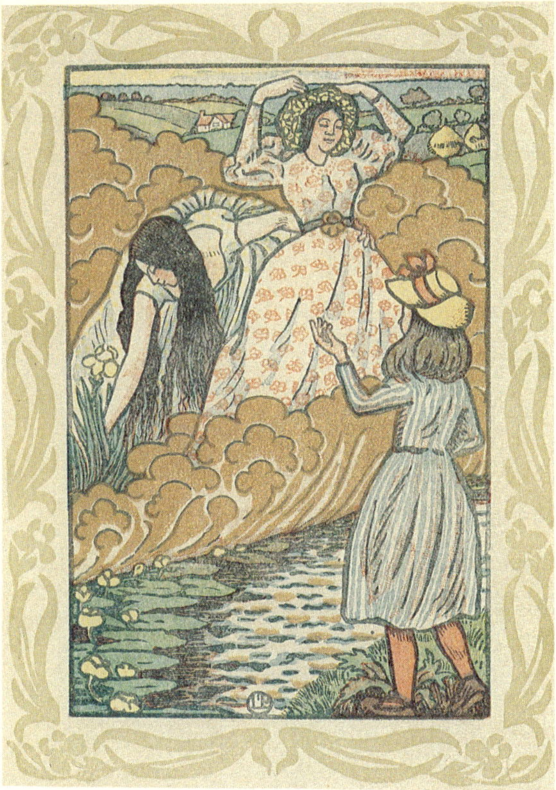

above Rust. The Queen of the Fishes (1894)

next page Ronsard. Choix de Sonnets (1902)

RONSARD.

CHOIX DE SONNETS.

OF GARDENS BY FRANCIS BACON.

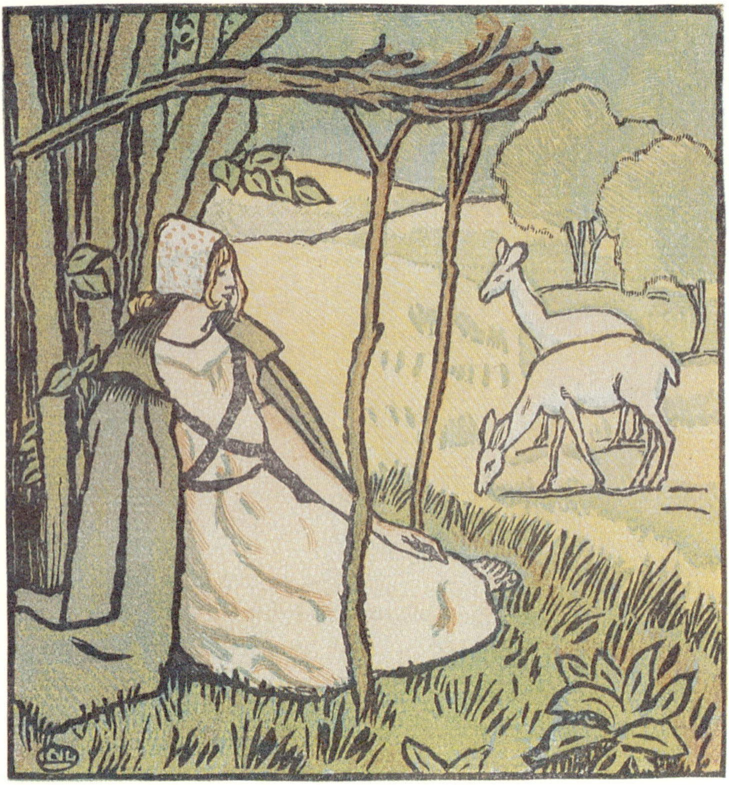

above C'est d'Aucassin et de Nicolete (1903)

opposite Keats. La Belle Dame sans Merci (1906)

previous page Bacon. Of Gardens (1902)

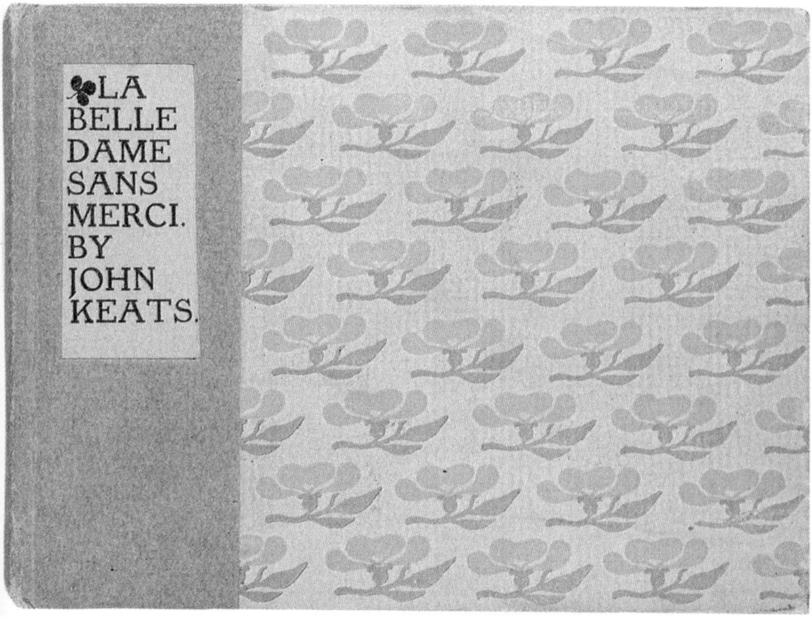
LA
BELLE
DAME
SANS
MERCI.
BY
JOHN
KEATS.

RONSARD.

ABREGE DE L'ART POETIQUE.

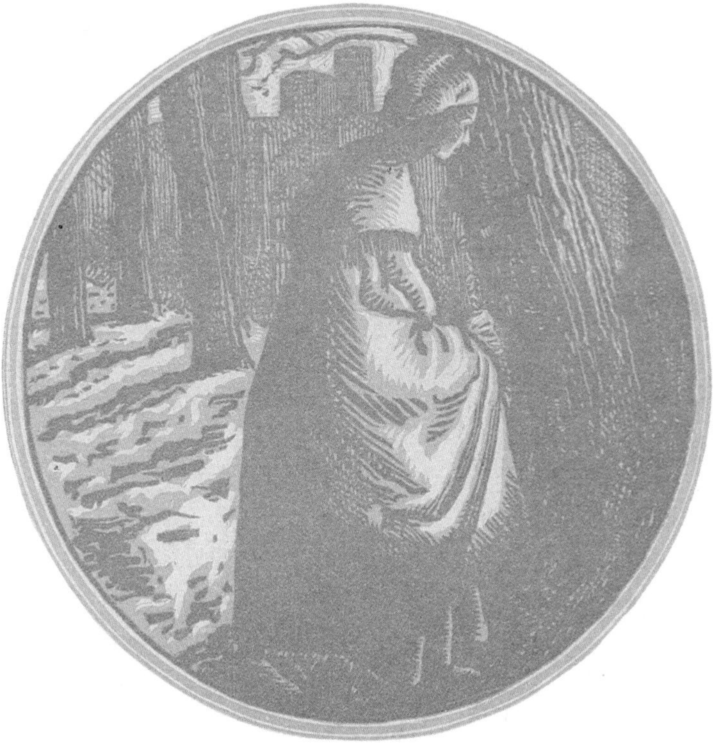

above Coleridge. *Christabel, Kubla Khan, Fancy in Nubibus, and Song from Zapolya* (1904)

previous page Ronsard. *Abrégé de l'Art Poetique Français* (1903)

CHRISTABEL,
KUBLA KHAN,
FANCY IN NUBI-
BUS, & A SONG,
BY SAMUEL T.
COLERIDGE.

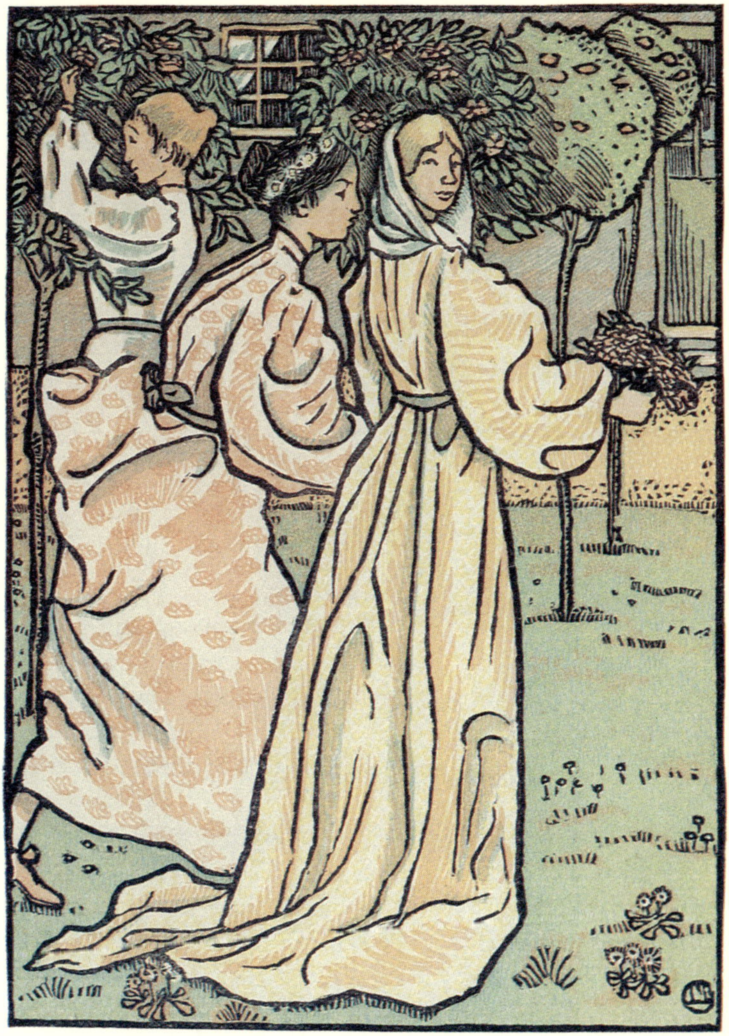

above Browning. Some Poems by Robert Browning (1904)

opposite Coleridge. Christabel, Kubla Khan, Fancy in Nubibus, and Song from Zapolya (1904)

DREAM,
COME,
TRUE.
BY
L. BINYON.

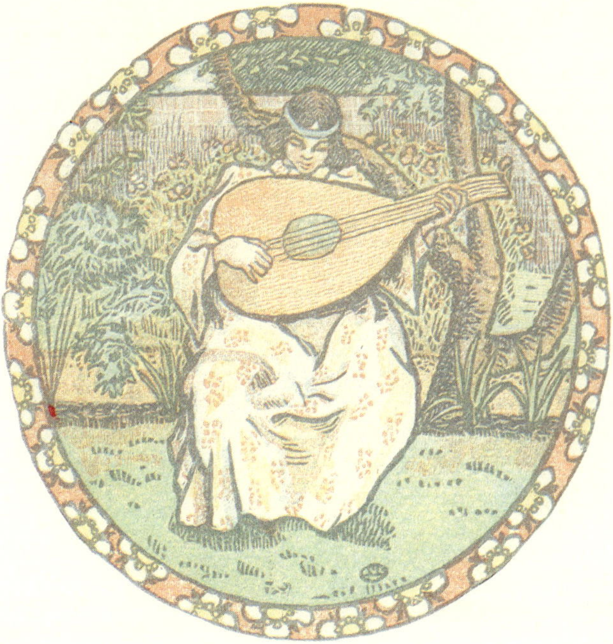

above Steele. *Some Old French and English Ballads* (1905)

opposite Binyon. *Dream Come True* (1905)

next page Moore. *The Little School, a Posy of Rhymes* (1905)

THE LITTLE SCHOOL. BY T. STURGE MOORE.

HISTOIRE DE LA REINE DU MATIN & DE SOLIMAN PRINCE DES GÉNIES.

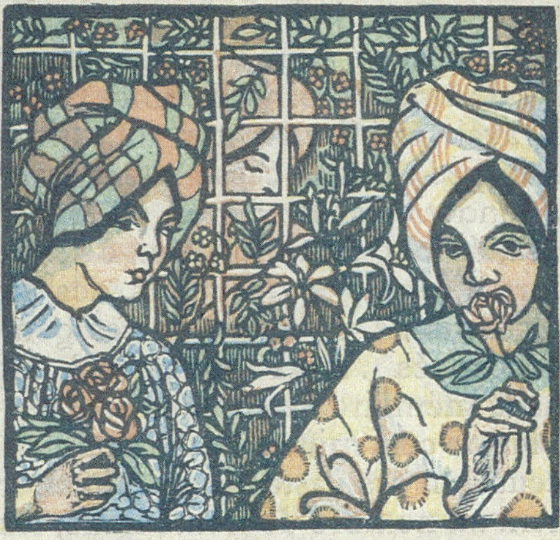

I. ADONIRAM.

POUR servir les desseins du grand roi Soliman Ben-Daoud, son serviteur Adoniram avait renoncé depuis

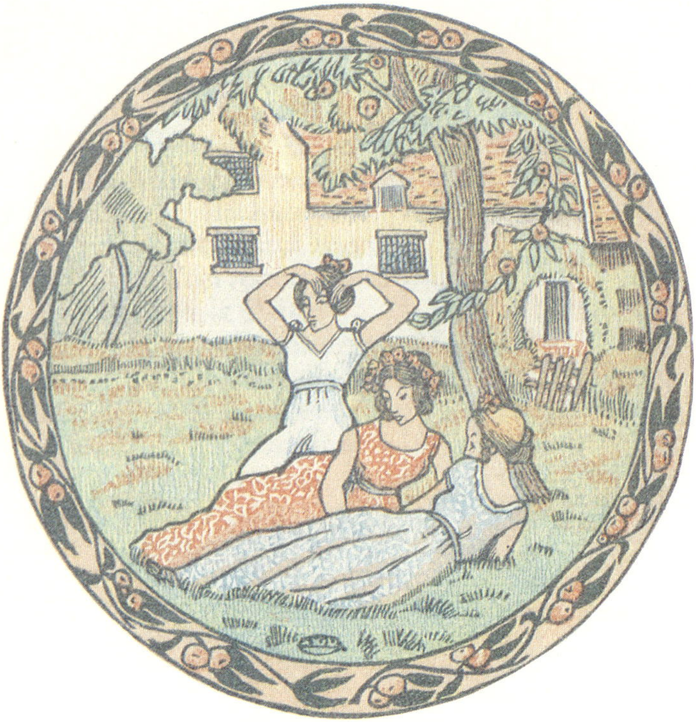

above Jonson. *Songs by Ben Jonson* (1906)

previous page Nerval. *Histoire de la Reine du Matin et de Soliman Ben Daoud* (1909)

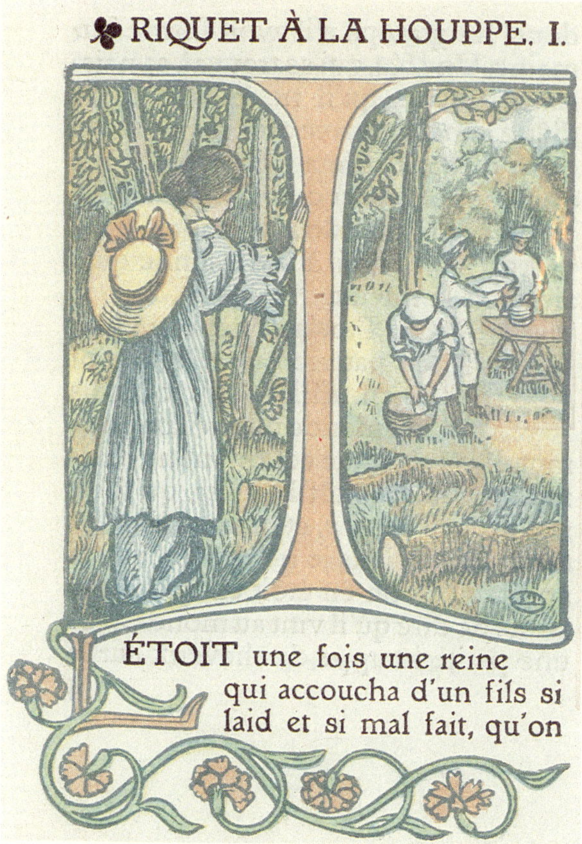

RIQUET À LA HOUPPE. I.

IL ÉTOIT une fois une reine qui accoucha d'un fils si laid et si mal fait, qu'on

Perrault. *Riquet a la Houppe* (1907)

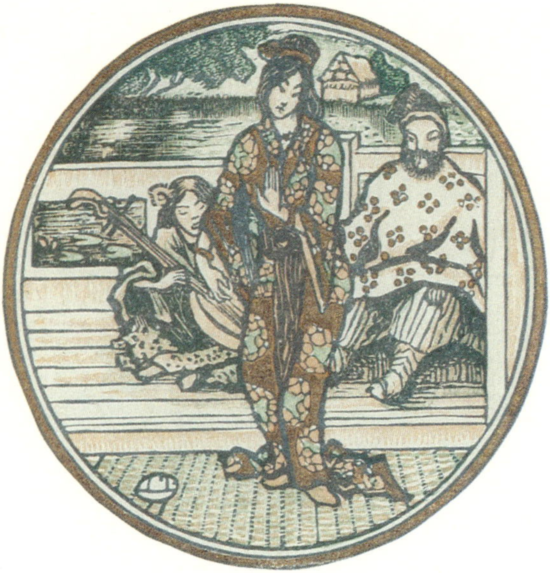

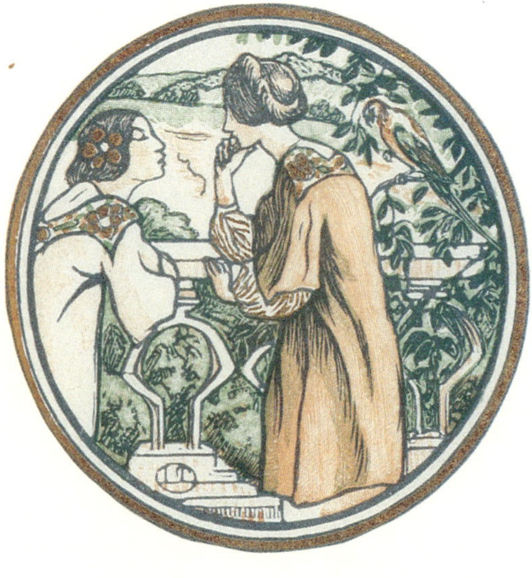

Gautier. Poems Tires du Livre de Jade, Ivresse d'Amour (1911)
Gautier. Poems Tires du Livre de Jade, Dans le Palais (1911)

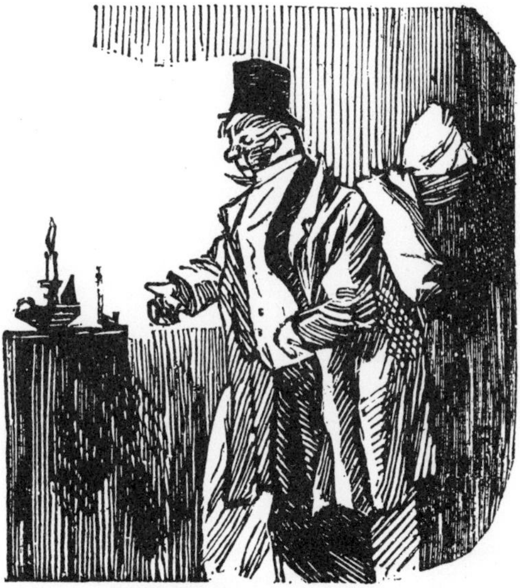

3. Copie de Ch. Keene (c.1885)

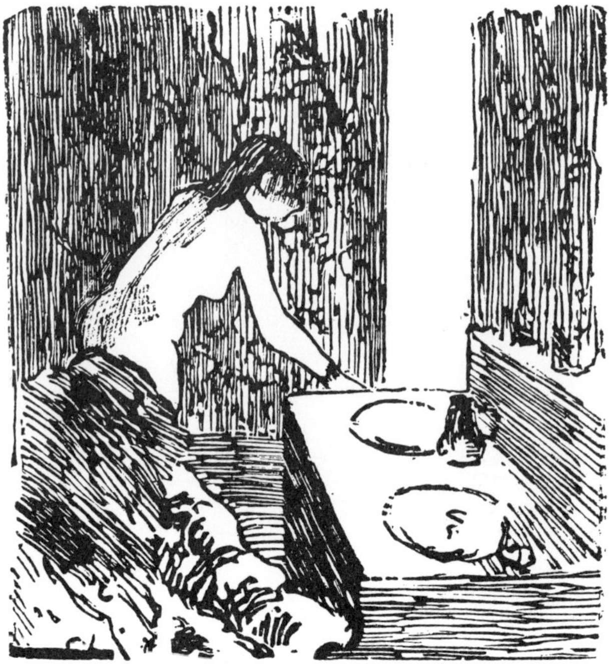

4. *The Bath* after Degas (c.1886)

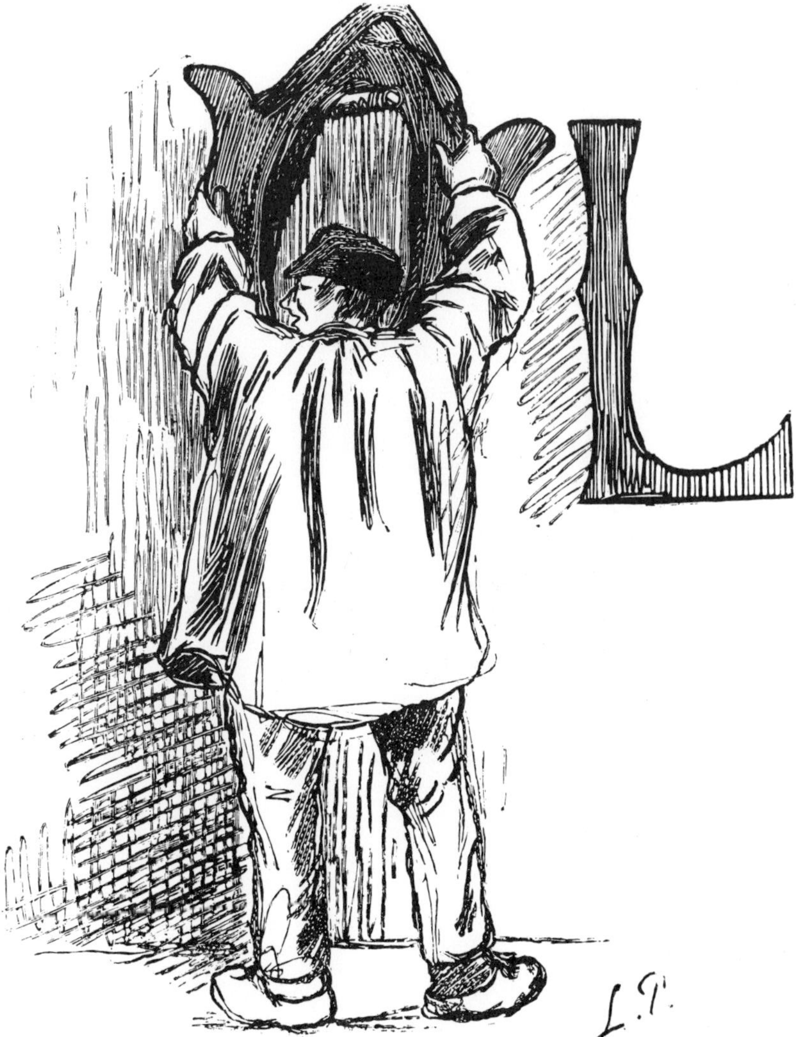

5. Mirbeau *Les Infortunes de Mait' Liziard* (1886) reduced

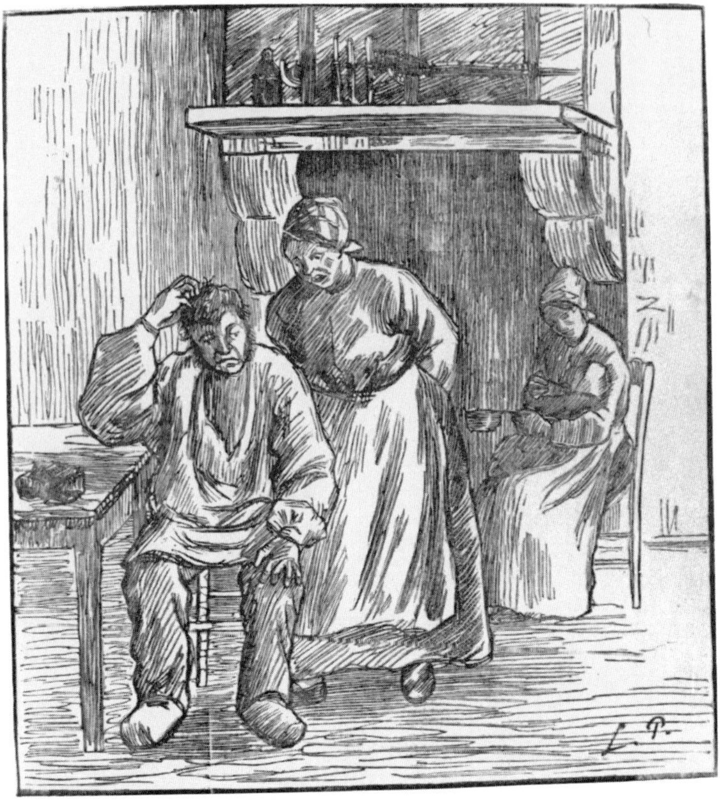

6. Mirbeau *Les Infortunes de Mait' Liziard* (1886)

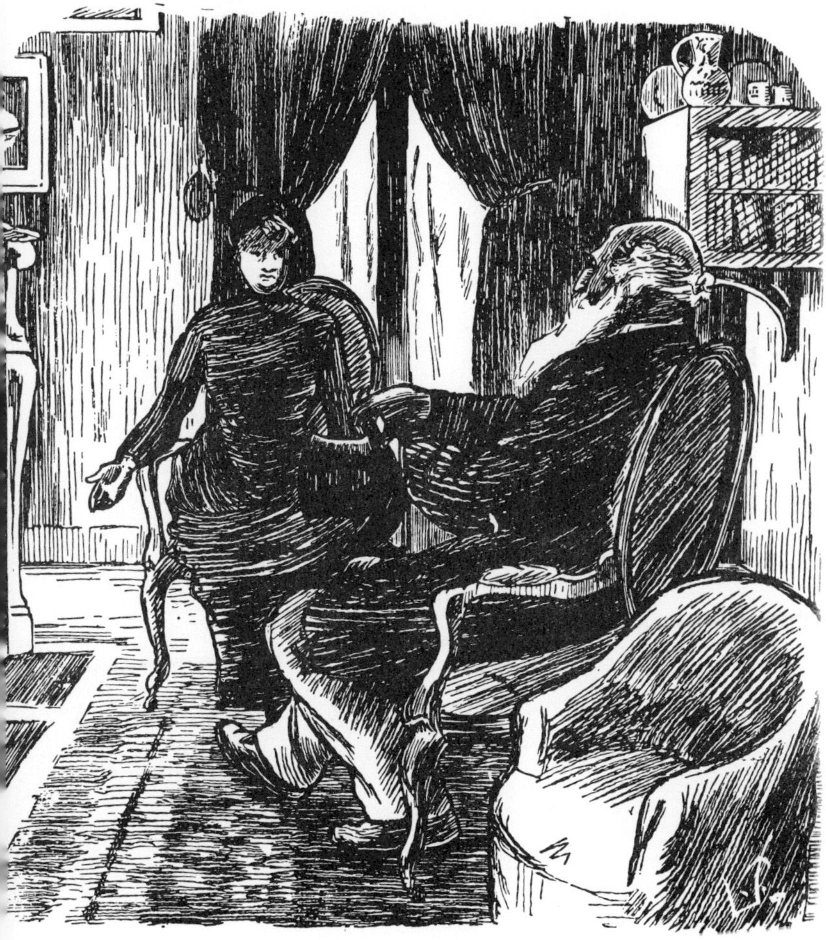

7. *La Visite* (c. 1886)

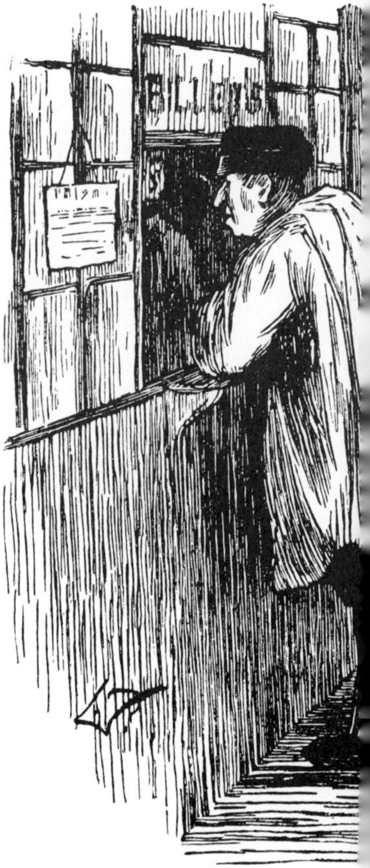
BILLETS

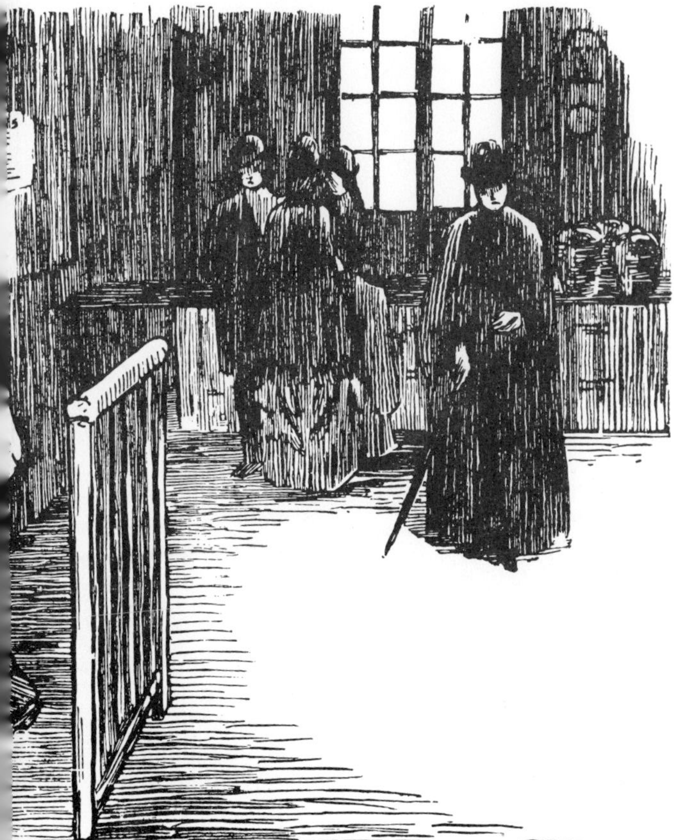

8. *La Gare* (1886)

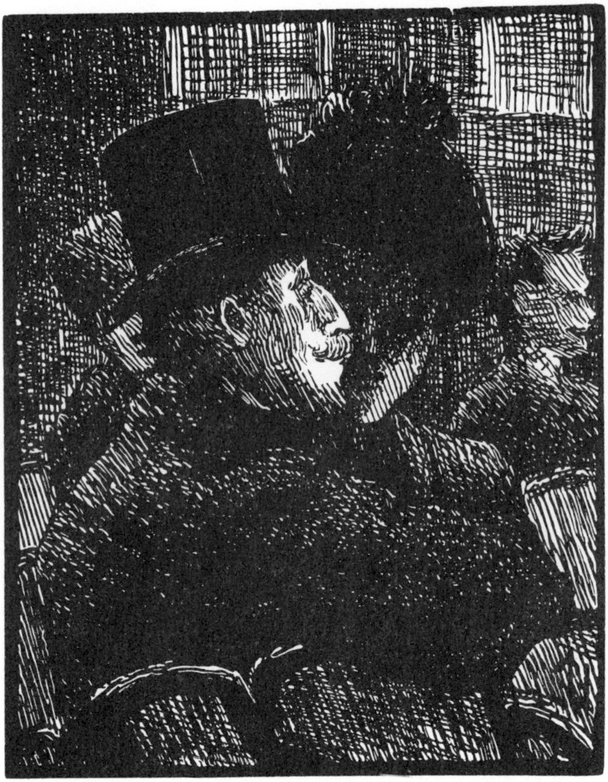

9. *Au Café-Concert* (1890)

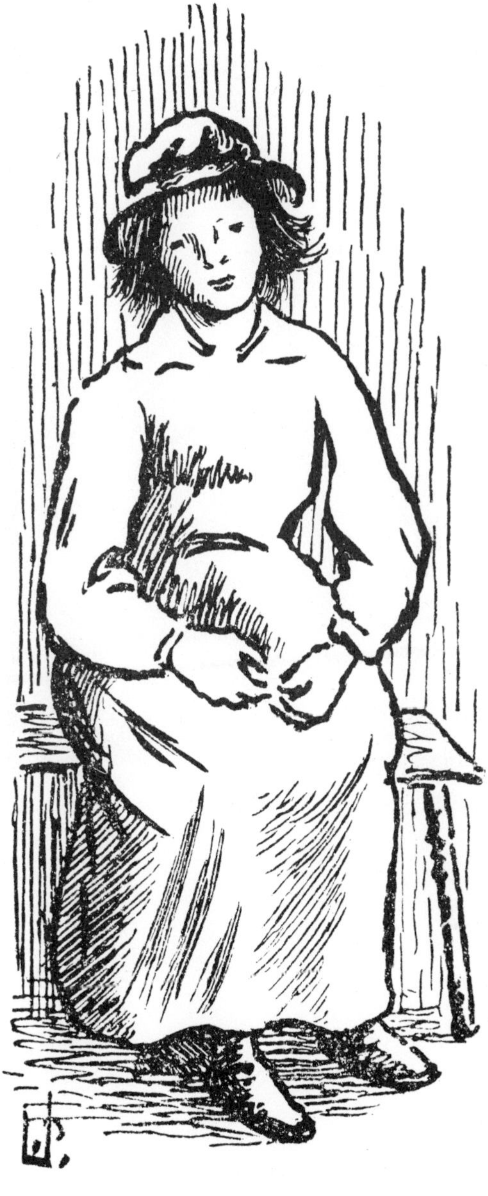

10. *Jeune Fille* (c. 1889)

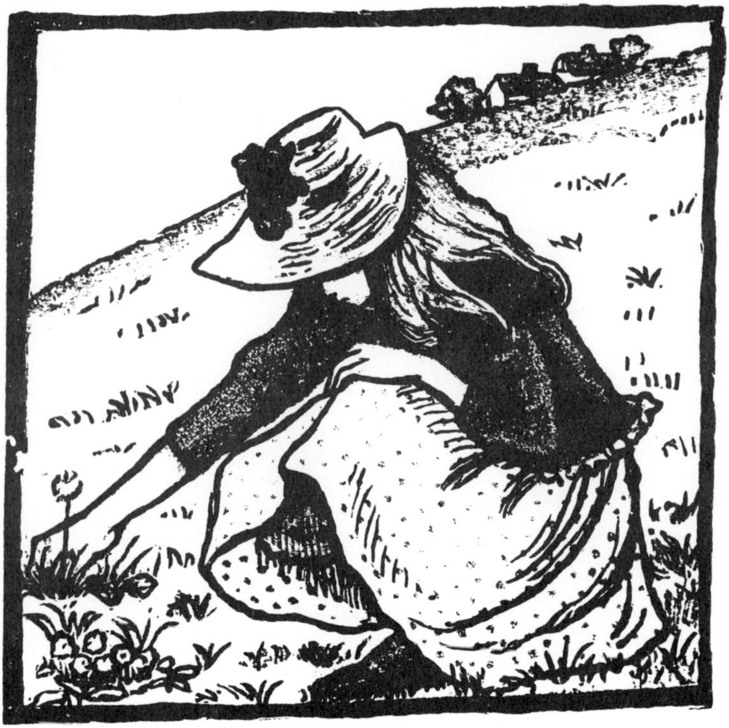

11. *Little May* (c. 1890)

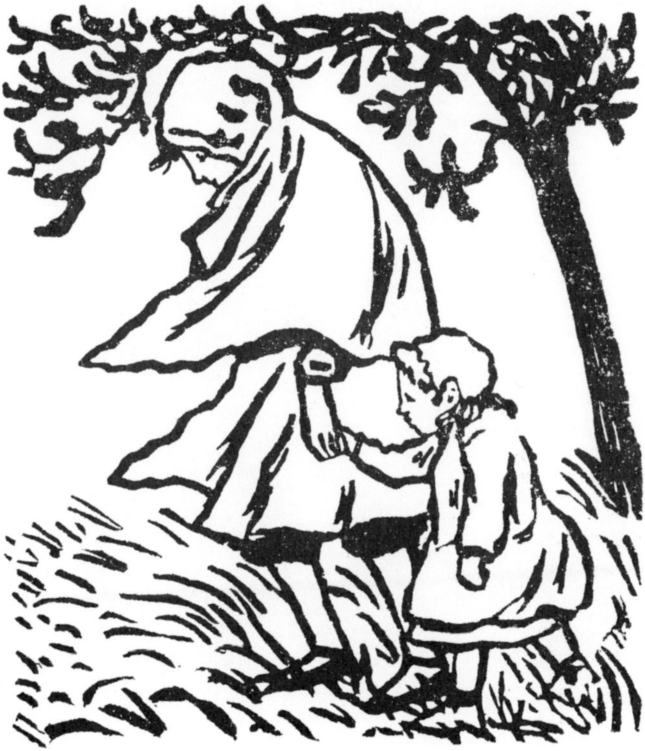

12. *April* (c. 1890)

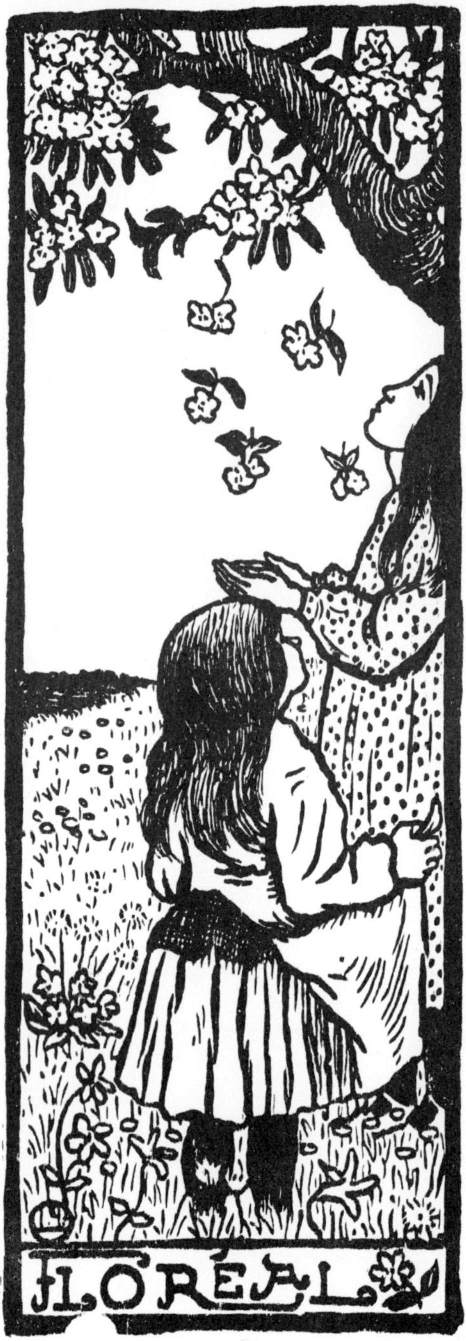

13. *Floreal* (1890)

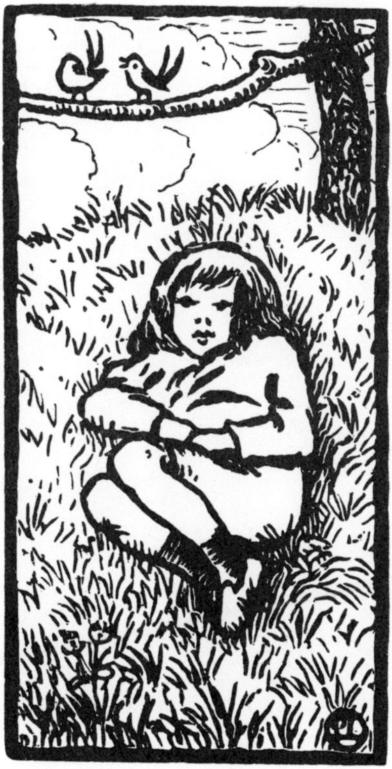

14. Contentment (1890)

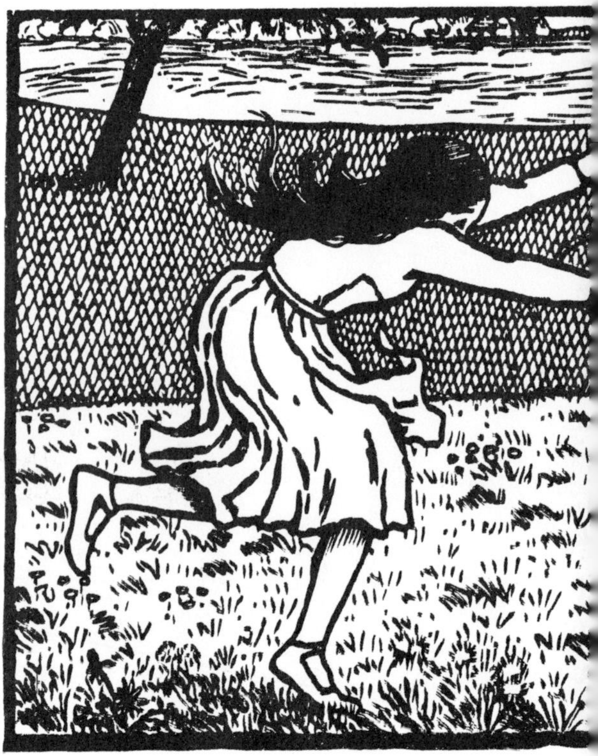

15. *Le Tennis* (1890)

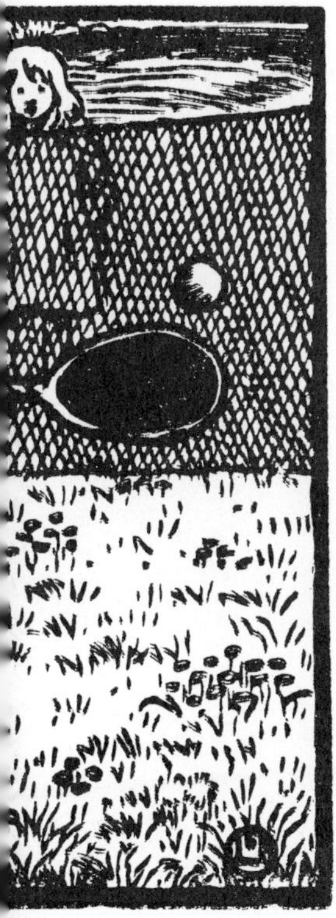

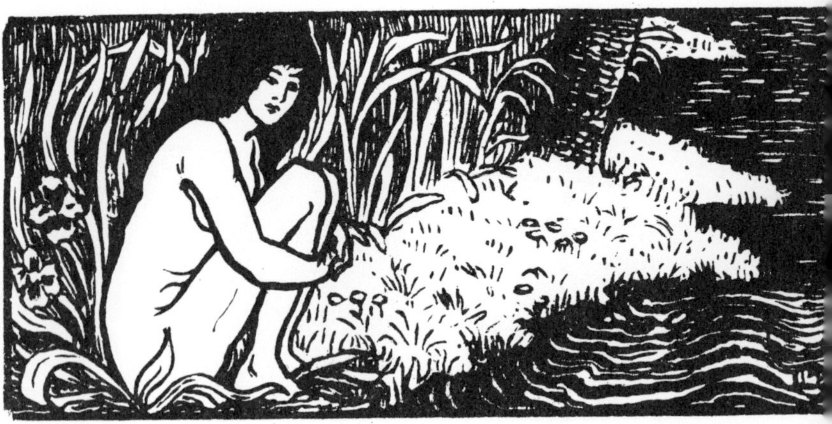

16. *Baigneuse* (1890)

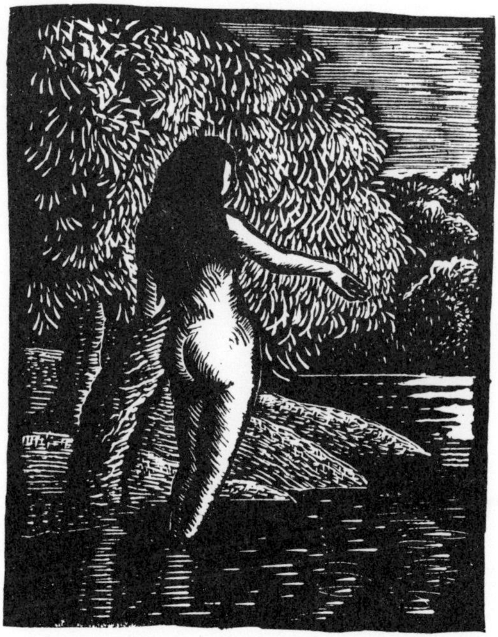

17. *Femme au bois* (c. 1891)

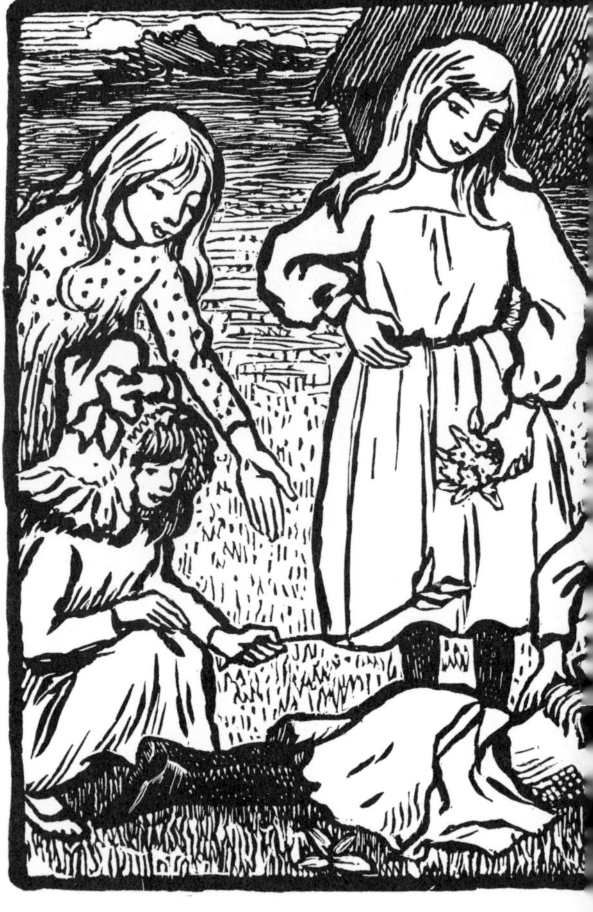

18. Enfants jouant (c. 1891)

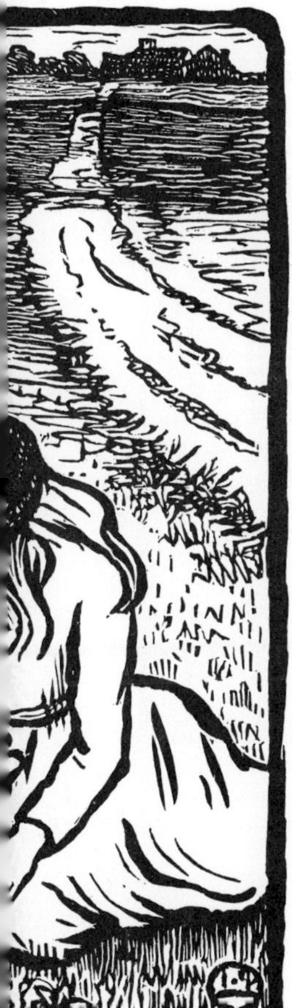

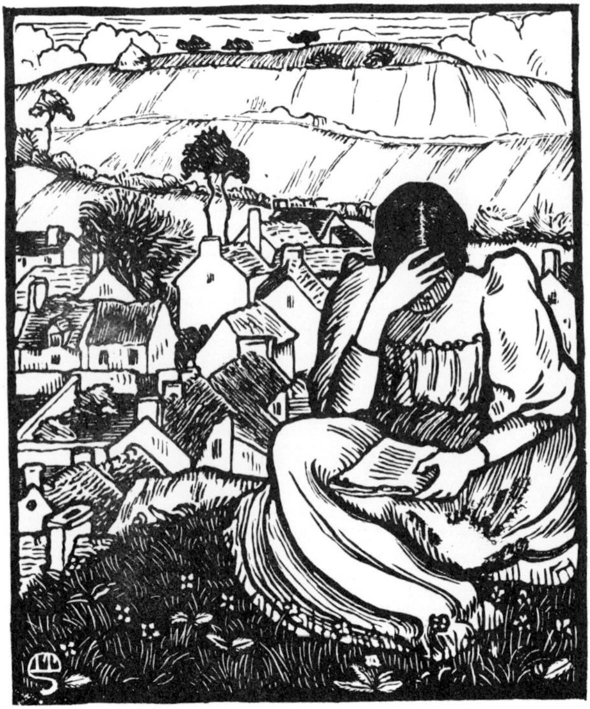

19. *Liseuse* (c. 1891)

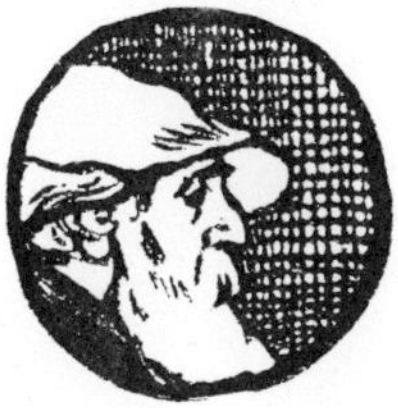

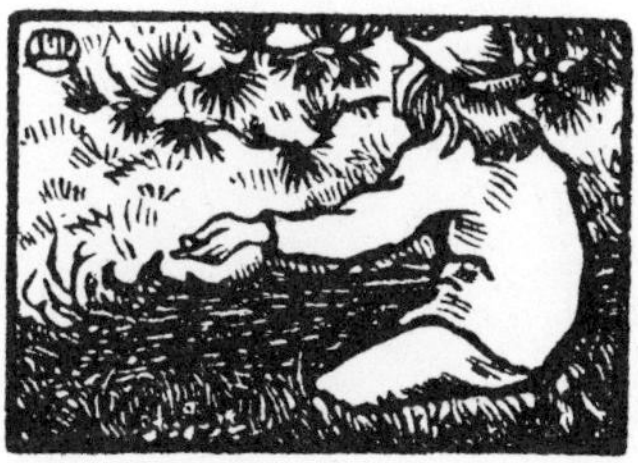

20. Portrait de Camille Pissarro (1892)

21. Boy and Pine Tree (1894)

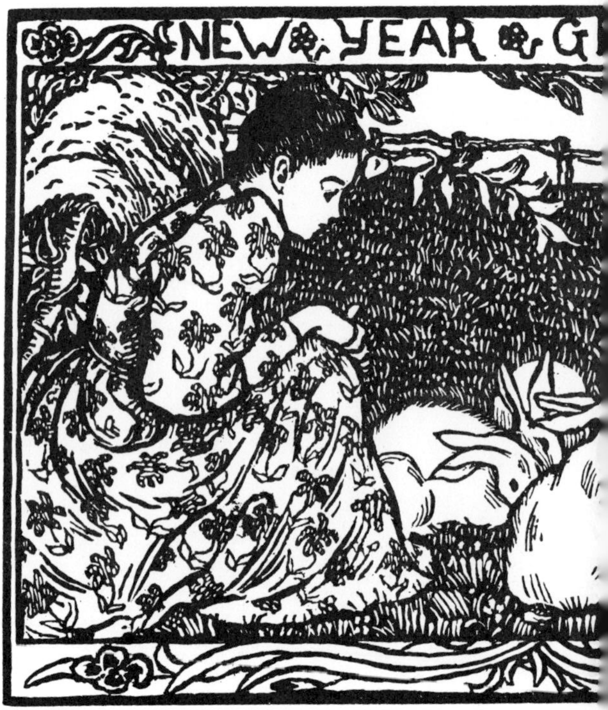

22. New Year Card (1893)

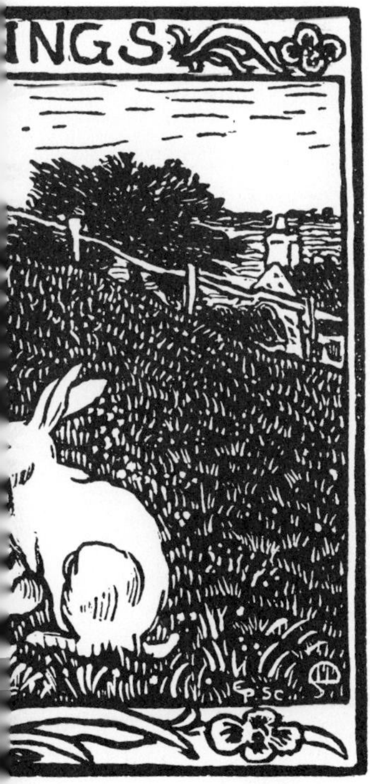
INGS

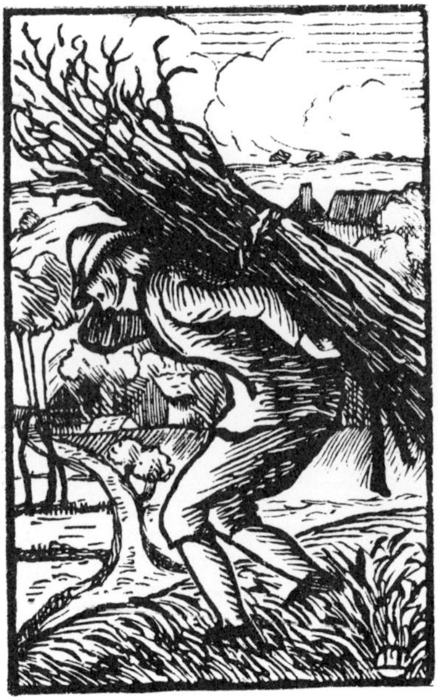

23. Rust The Queen of the Fishes (1894)

The Queen of the Fishes.

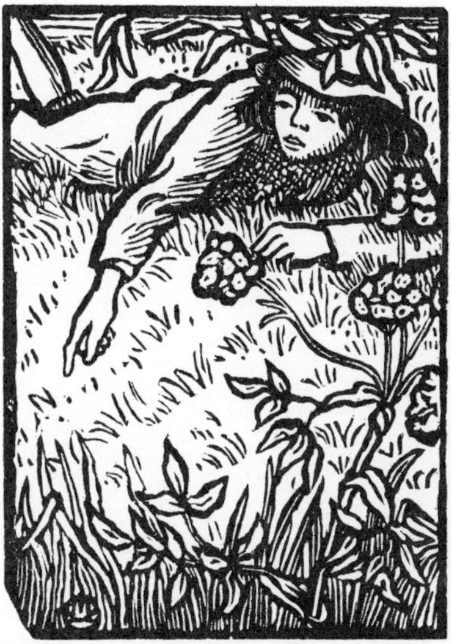

branches pointing up, gold-tipped, to the sky & out to the blue circle where the world ends. And looking down as he stood at the water's edge, he saw in the depths all the fishes of the river, the roach minnows & fierce old pike & all the great & little eels swimming & wriggling along in grand procession following a beautiful fish, her sides gleaming with scales of red red gold. As was his habit in the dream he cried «Ah, the QUEEN of the FISHES!» And he awoke. He sat up rubbing his eyes, & saw that it was evening & that the fairies

2

24. Rust The Queen of the Fishes (1894)

The Queen of the Fishes.

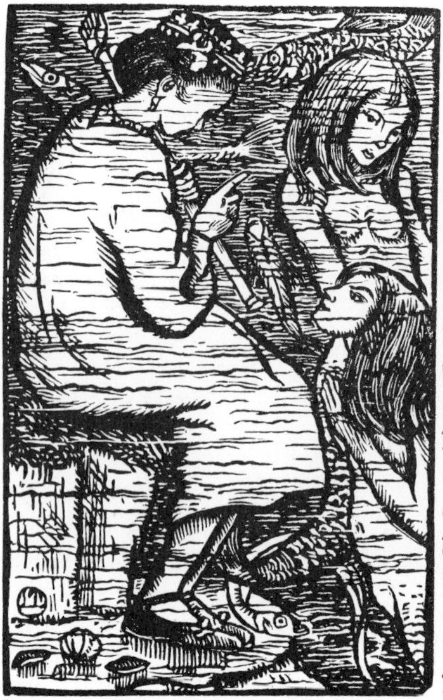

which seemed to them now only dreams. They had heard them often before yet he never tired of the story of her journeys under the clear water & the strange creatures & mermaids of her court where she was queen & how all the fishes swam about & played hide & seek with her in & out the water weeds. The boy seemed great & grand to the little fisher-girl

6

25. Rust The Queen of the Fishes (1894)

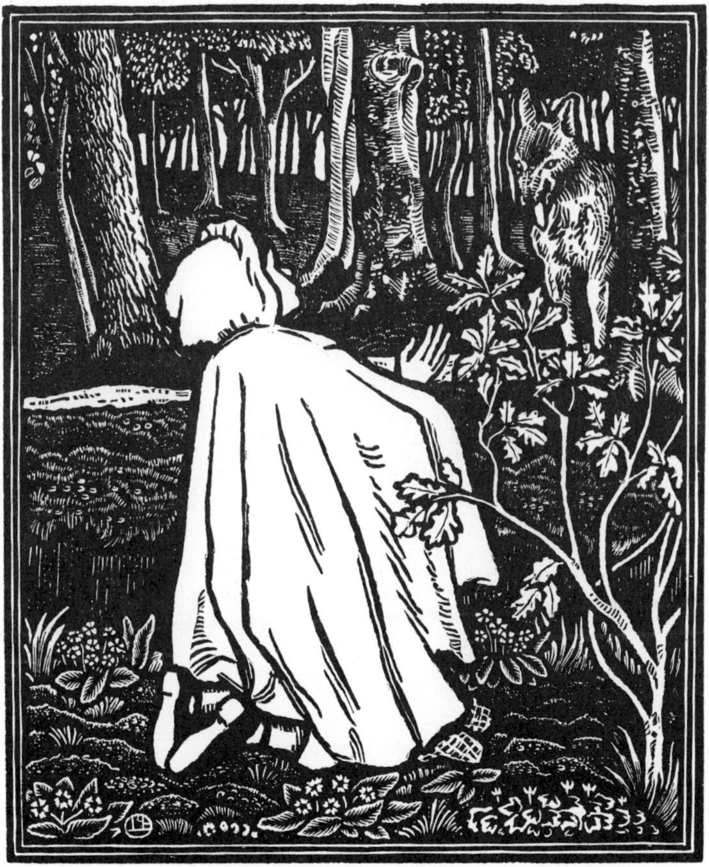

26. Le Petit Chaperon Rouge (c. 1895)

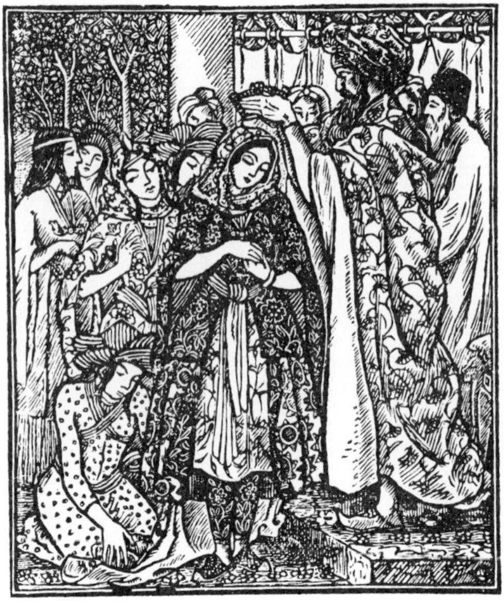

27. The Book of Ruth (1896)

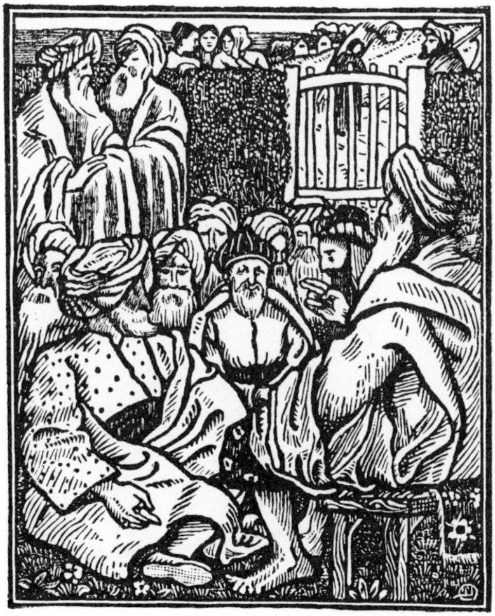

28. The Book of Ruth (1896)

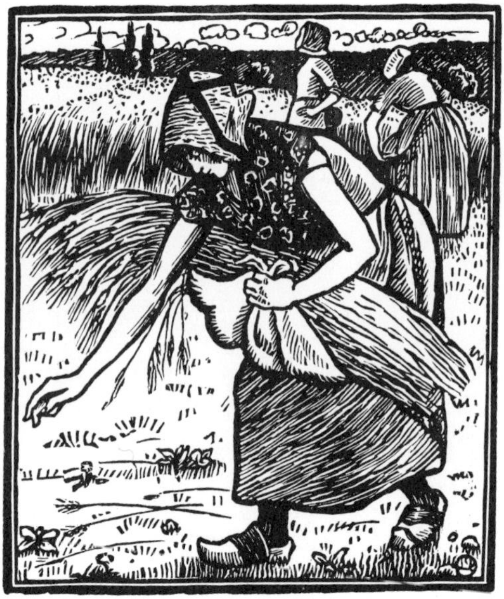

29. *The Book of Ruth* (1896)

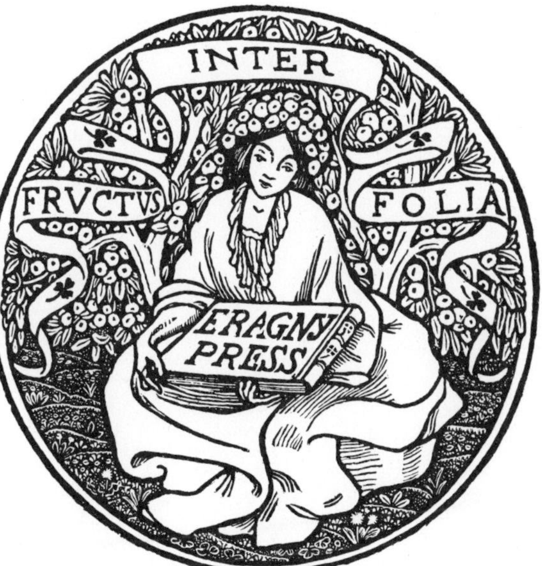

30. Press Mark II (1899)

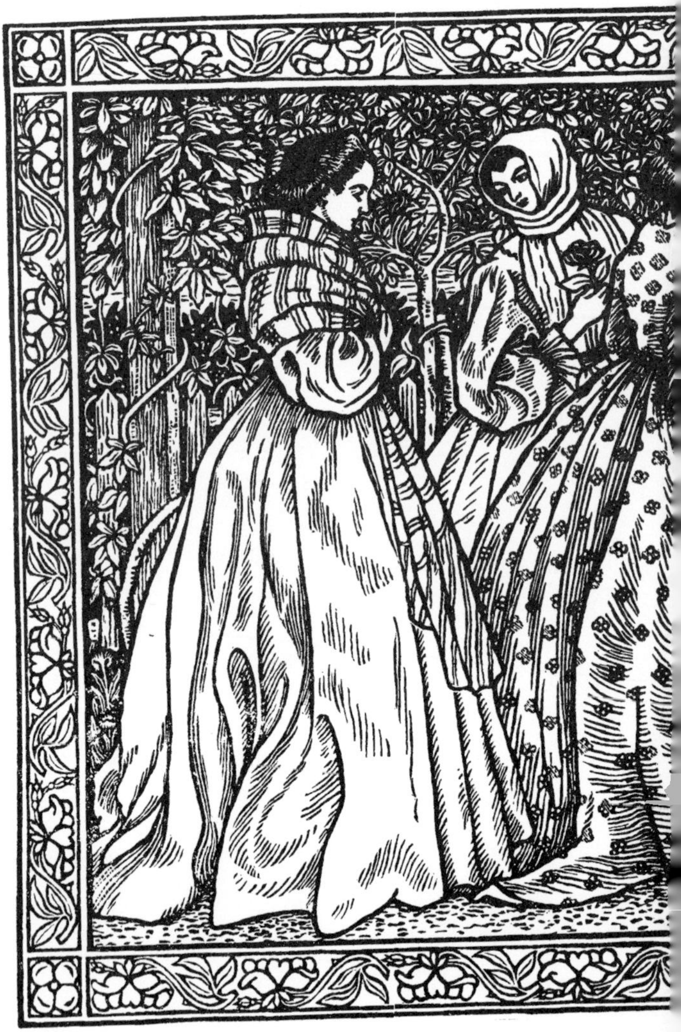

31. *Les Roses d'Antan* (1896)

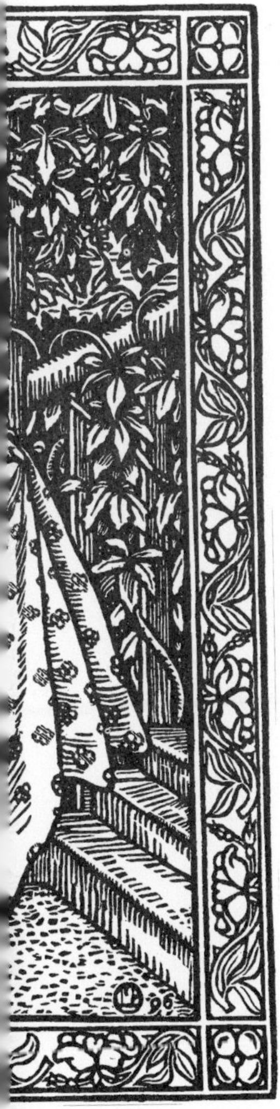

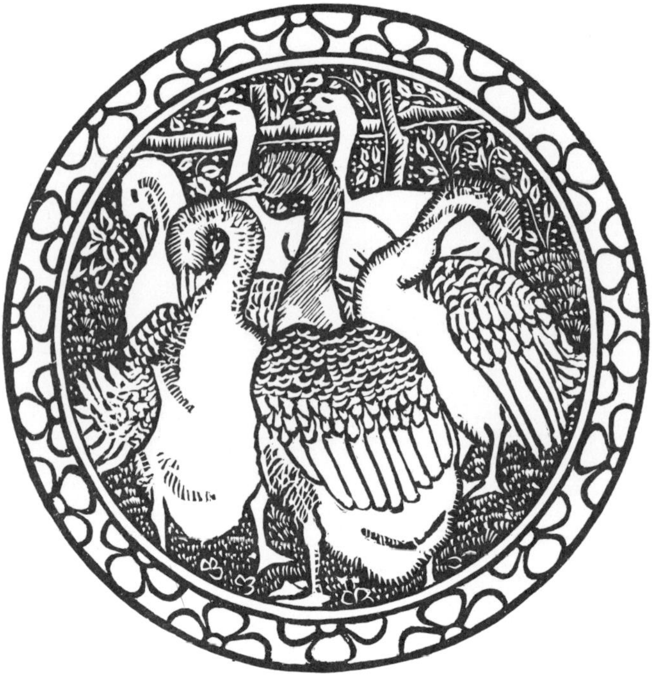

32. *Geese* (1899)

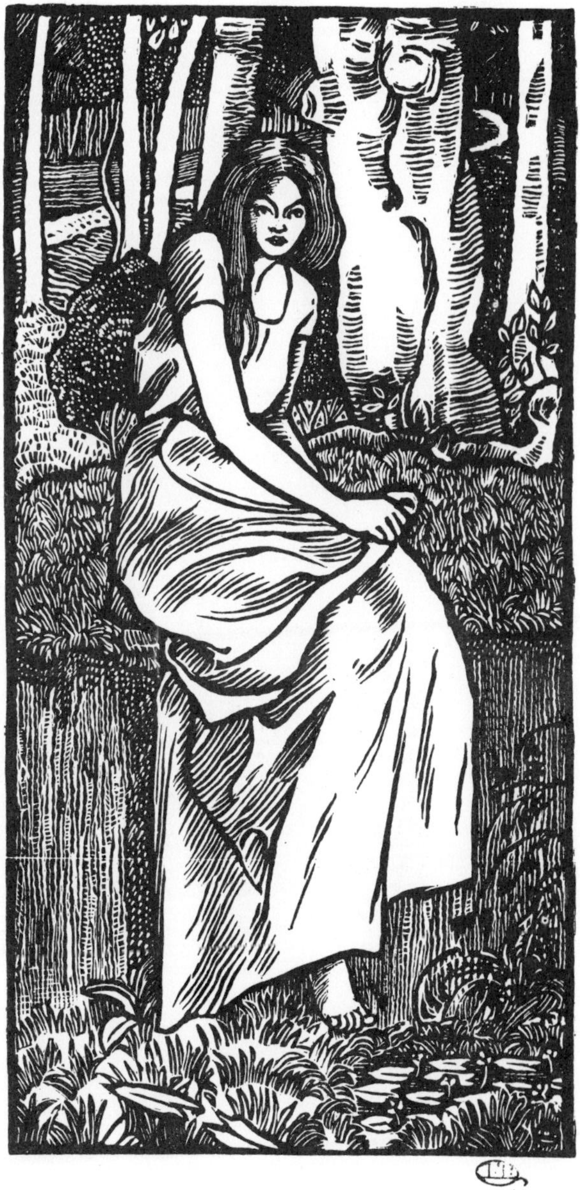

33. *Woodland Girl* (c. 1899)

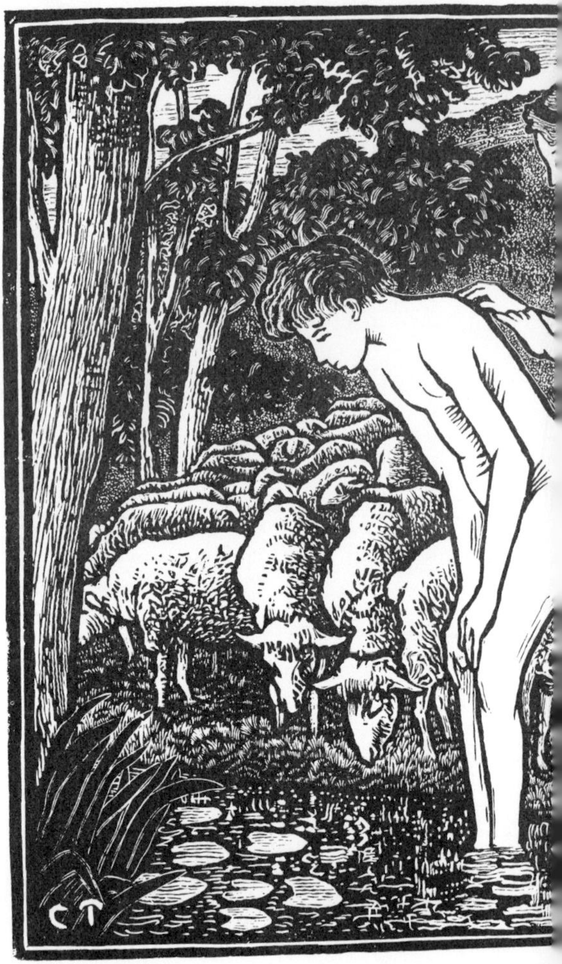

34. Daphnis et Chloë (c. 1899)

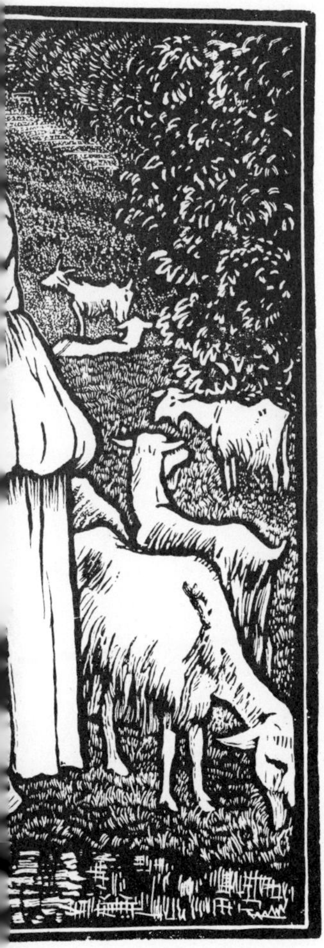

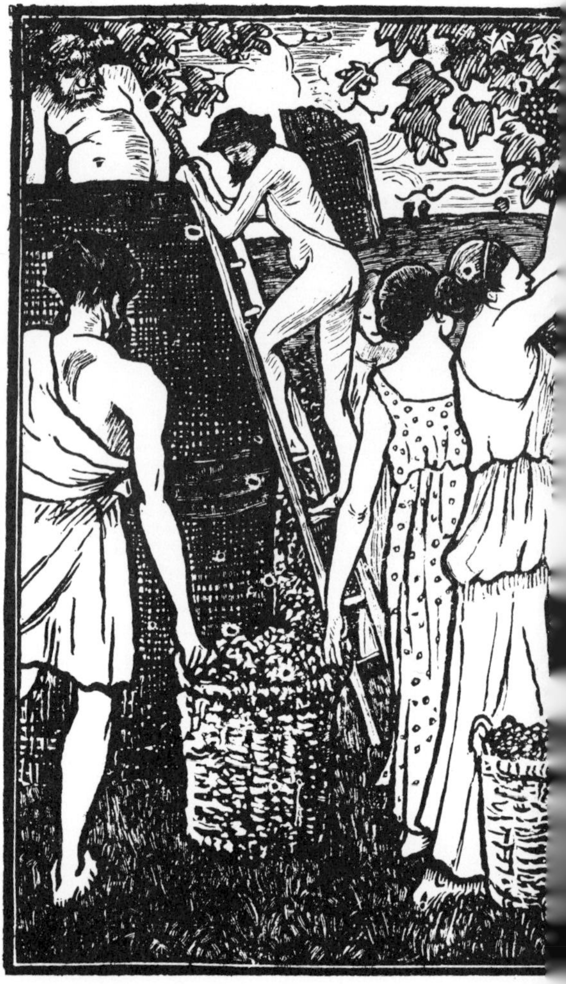

35. *Daphnis et Chloë* (c. 1899)

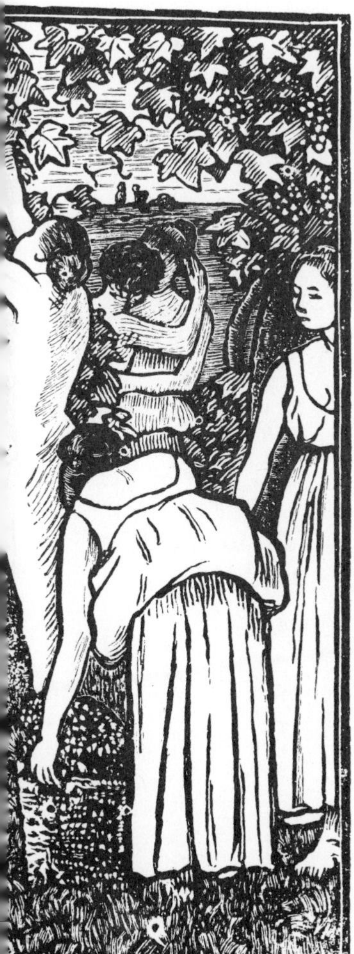

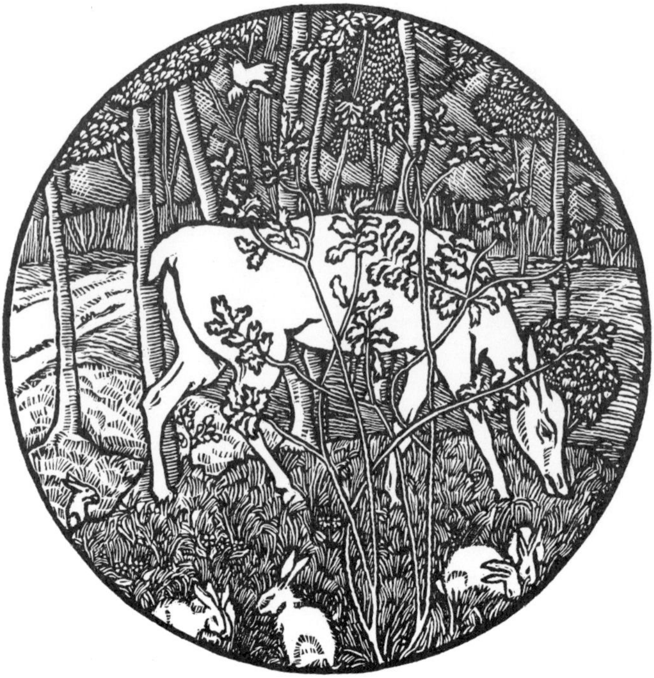

36. Flaubert *St Julien* (1900)

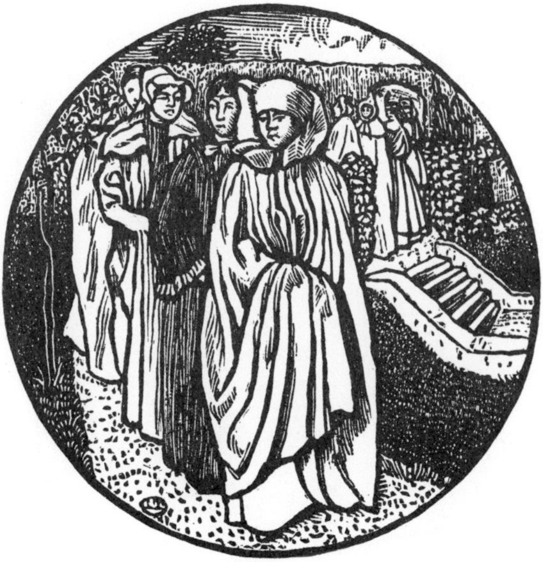

37. Villon *Les Ballades de Francois Villon* (1900)

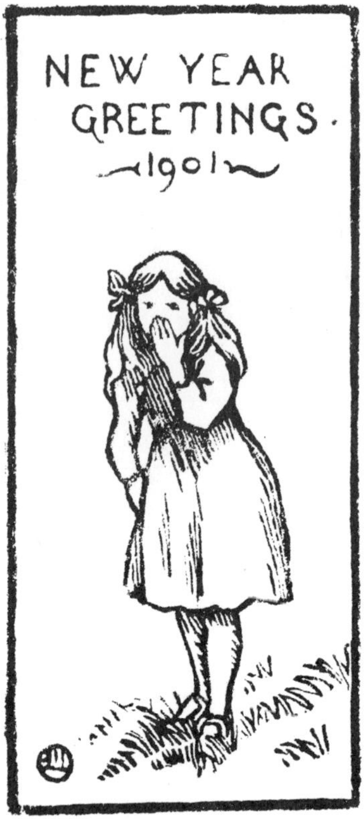

38. *New Year Card* (1901)

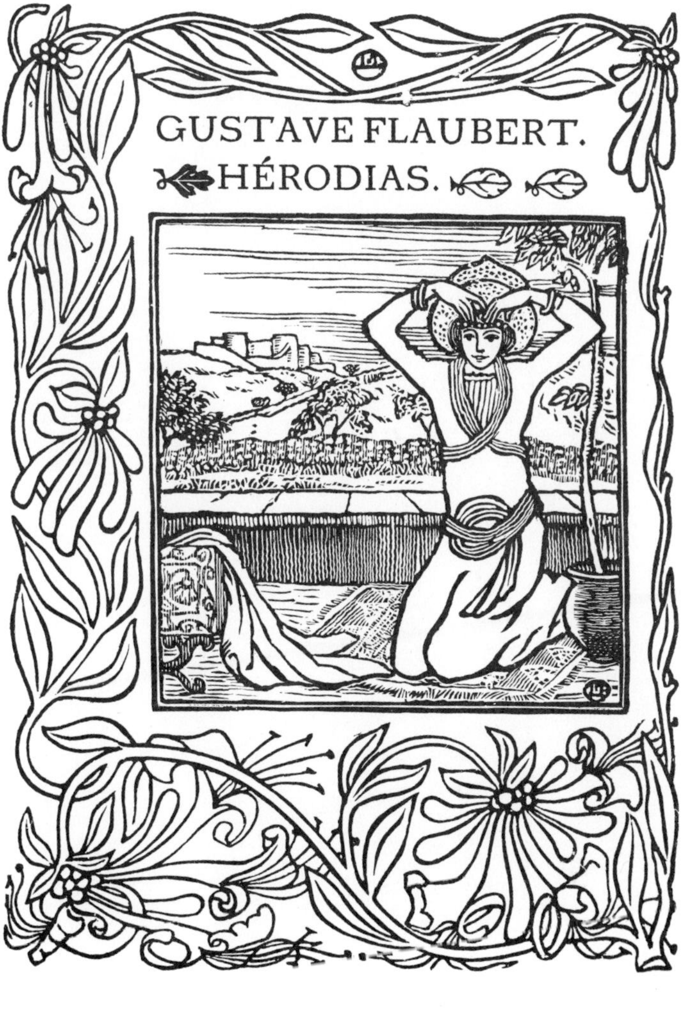

39. Flaubert *Herodias* (1901)

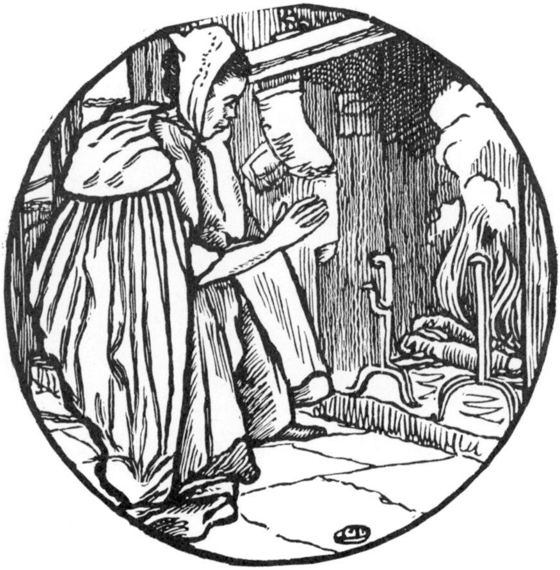

40. Villon *Autres Poésies* (1901)

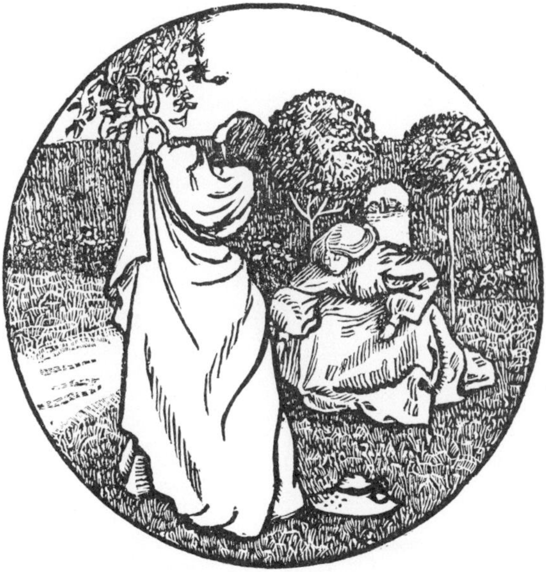

41. Bacon *Of Gardens* (1902)

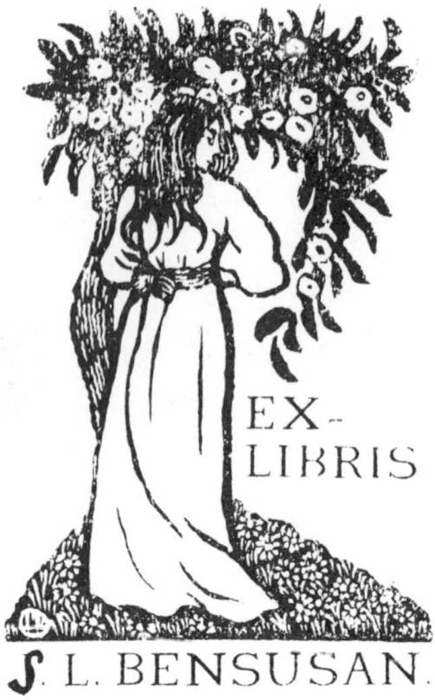

42. *Ex Libris* (c. 1901)

43. Perrault *Histoire de Peau d'Ane* (1902), illustration by T. Sturge Moore

HISTOIRE DE PEAU D'ANE PAR CHARLES PERRAULT.

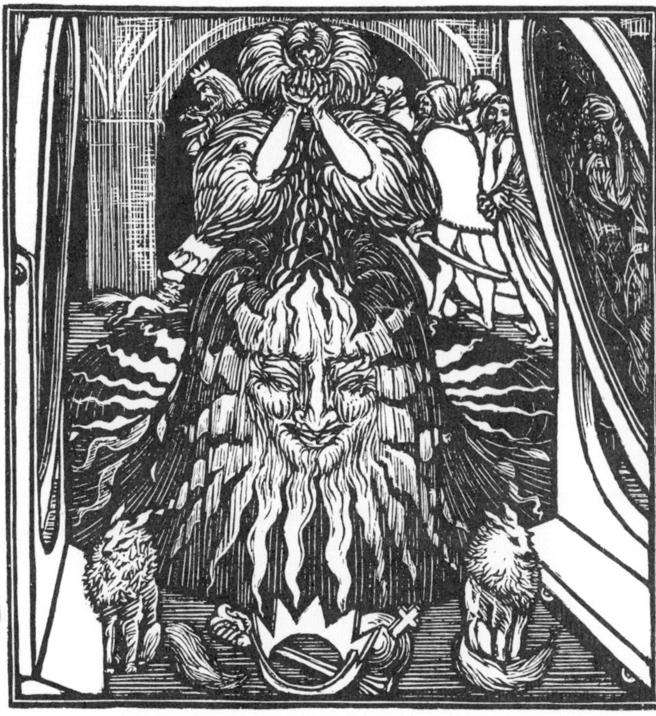

"Jamais on n'avait rien vu de si beau et de si artistement ouvré. (Page 18.)

IL ÉTAIT UNE FOIS UN ROI SI GRAND, SI AIMÉ DE SES PEUPLES, SI RES-

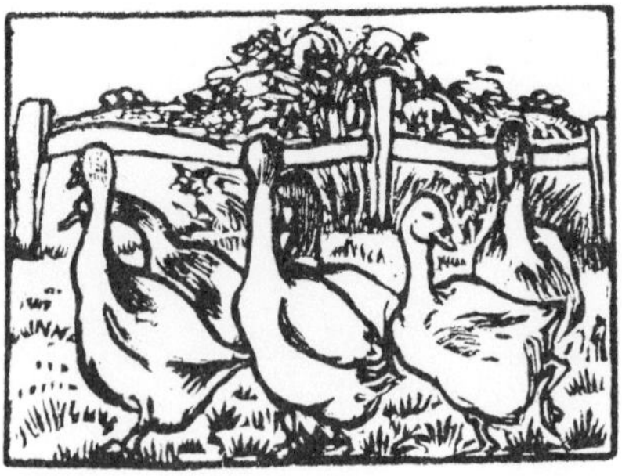

44. *Geese* (1903)

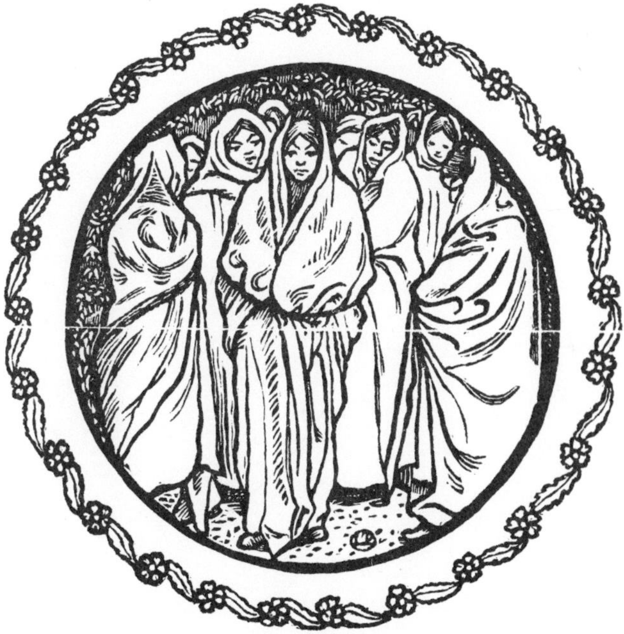

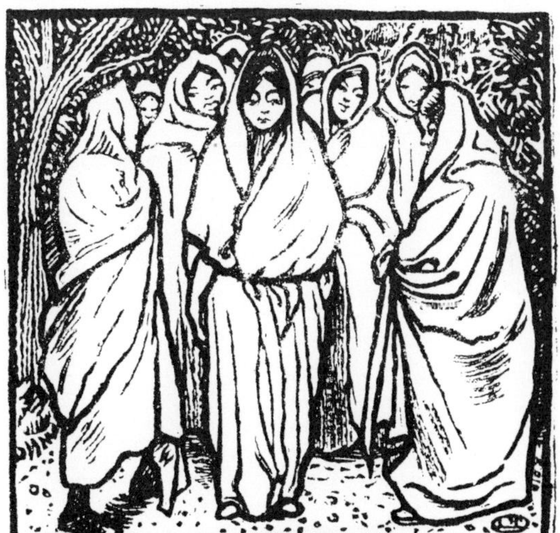

45. Consultation (1905)

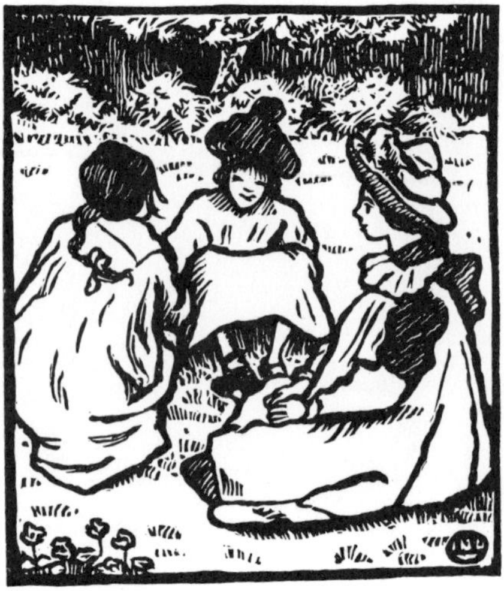

46. *Girls sitting on the grass* (1906)

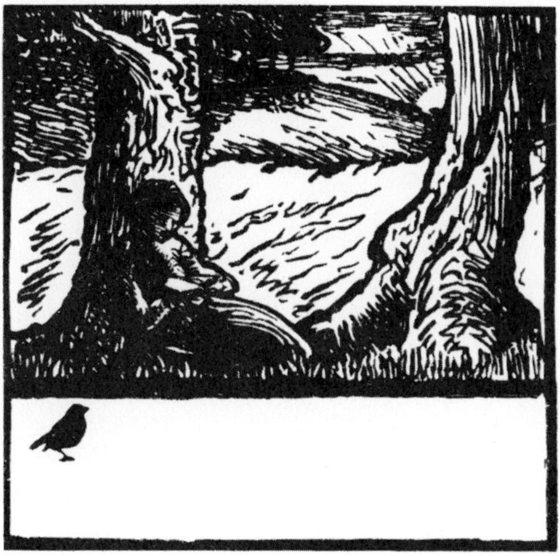

47. Bookplate & New Year card (1905)

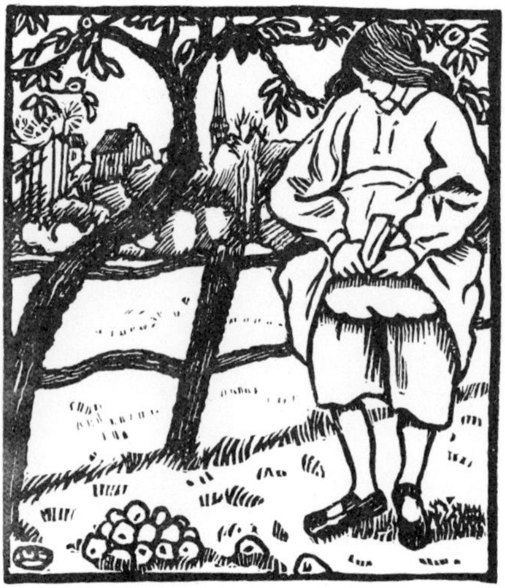

48. Boy gathering apples (1905)

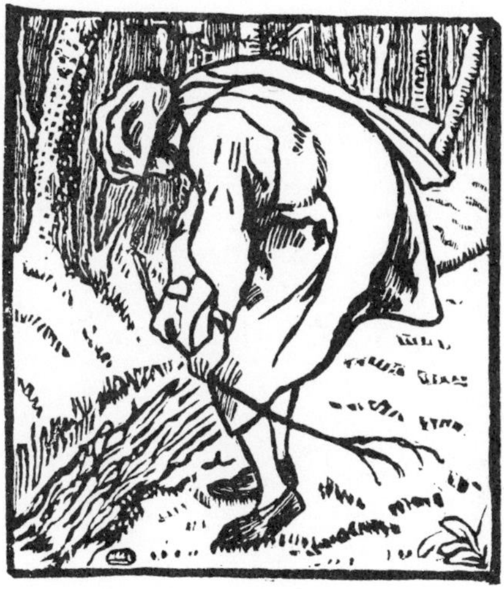

49. *Man breaking a stick* (1905)

VERSES BY CHRISTINA G. ROSSETTI.
DEDICATED TO HER MOTHER.

Perchè temer degg'io? Son le mie voci
Inesperte, lo so: ma il primo omaggio
D'accettarne la MADRE
Perciò non sdegnerà; ch' anzi assai meglio
Quanto a lei grata io sono
L'umil dirà semplicità del dono.

Metastasio.

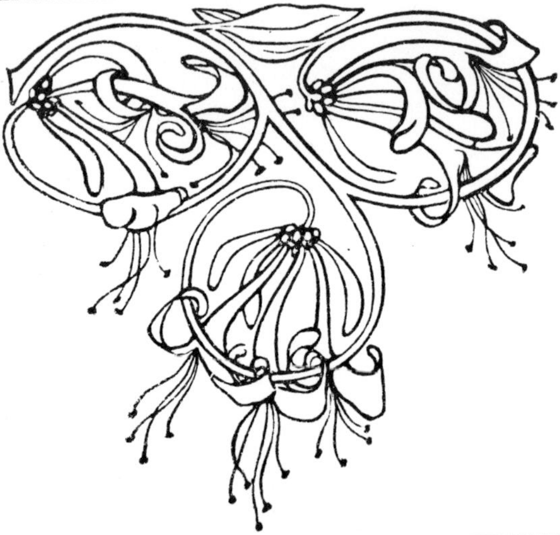

Privately printed at G. Polidori's, No. 15 Park Village East, Regent's Park, London. 1847.

50. *Verses* by Christina Rossetti (1906)

VERSES BY CHRISTINA G. ROSSETTI

THE DEAD CITY.

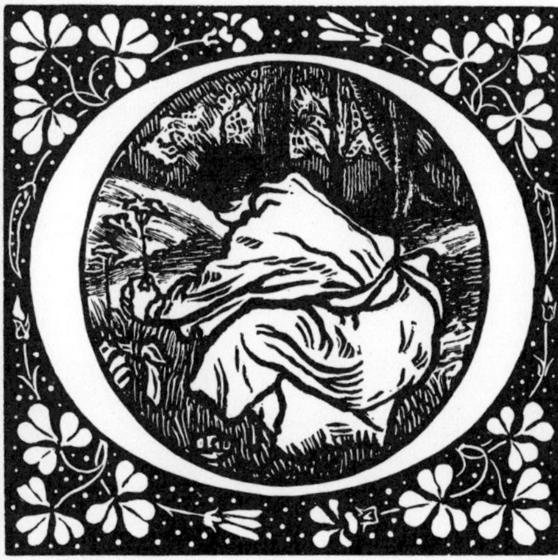

ONCE I RAMBLED IN A WOOD WITH A CARELESS HARDIHOOD HEEDING NOT THE TANGLED WAY;
LABYRINTHS AROUND ME LAY,
BUT FOR THEM I NEVER STOOD.

On, still on, I wandered on,
And the sun above me shone;
And the birds around me winging
With their everlasting singing
Made me feel not quite alone.

In the branches of the trees
Murmured like the hum of bees
The low sound of happy breezes,
Whose sweet voice that never ceases
Lulls the heart to perfect ease.

51. *Verses by Christina Rossetti* (1906)

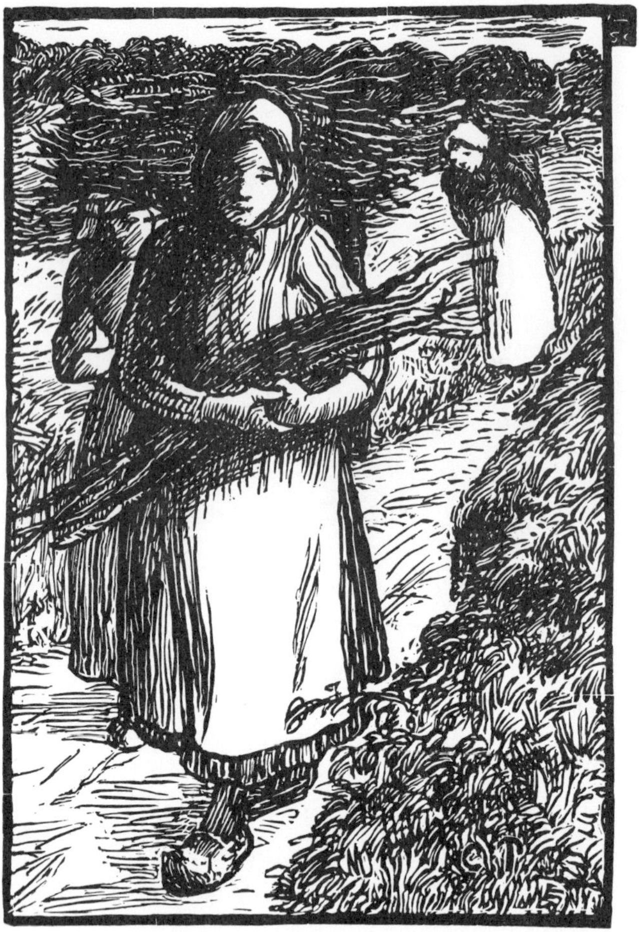

52. *Porteuses de Fagot* after Camille Pissarro (1908)

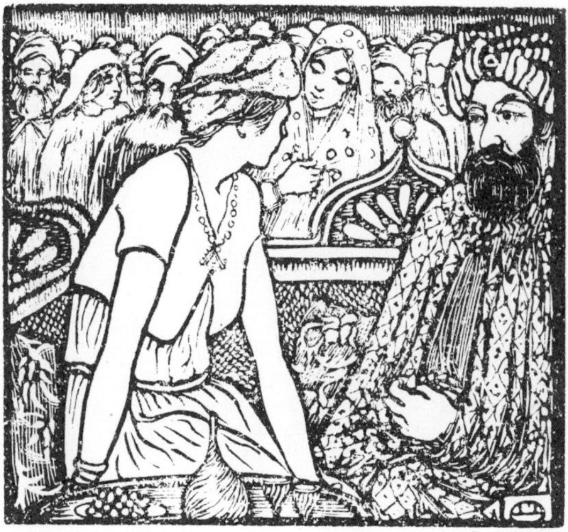

53. Nerval Histoire de la Reine du Matin et de Soliman Ben Daoud (1908)

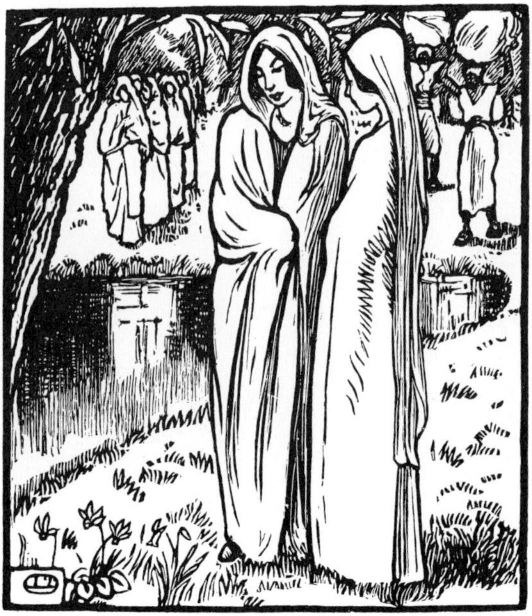

54. Nerval *Histoire de la Reine du Matin et de Soliman Ben Daoud* (1909)

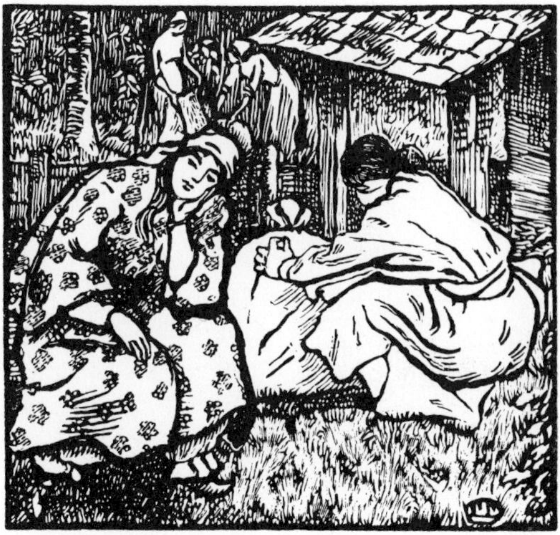

55. Nerval *Histoire de la Reine du Matin et de Soliman Ben Daoud*(1909)

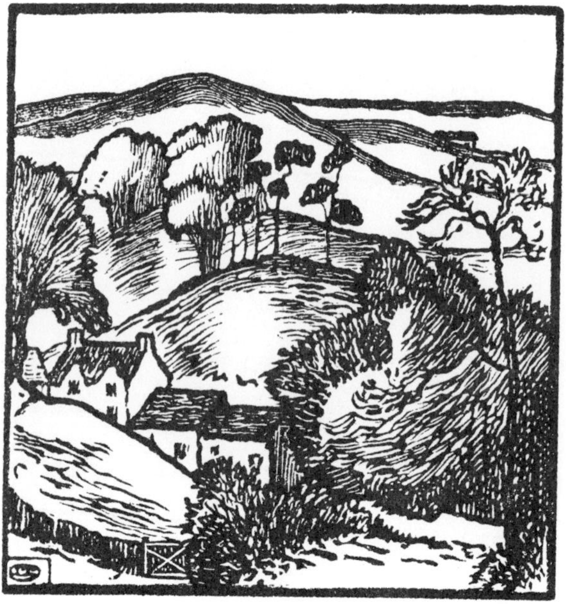

Landscape: Blackpool Devon (1914)

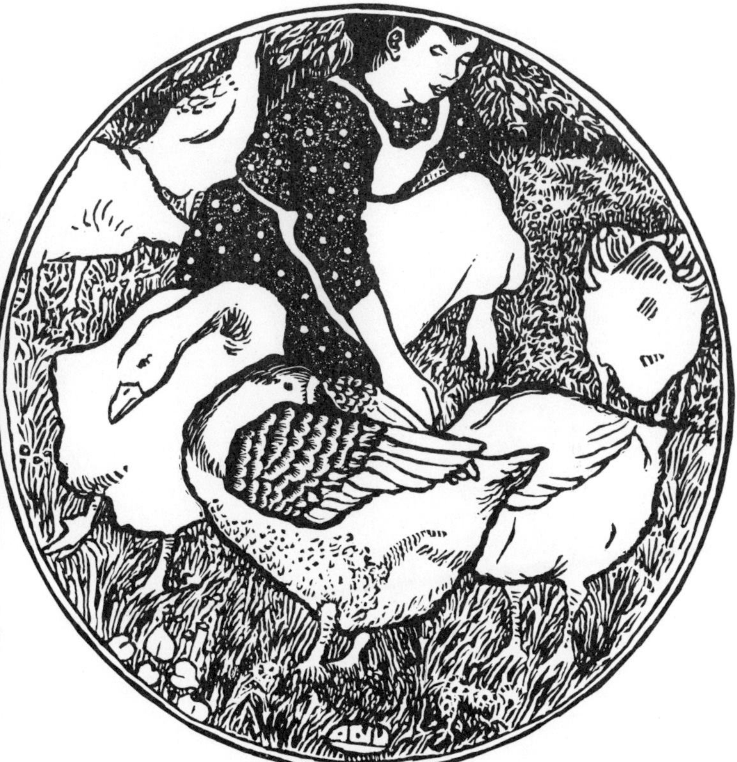

57. Gardeuse d'Oies (1923)

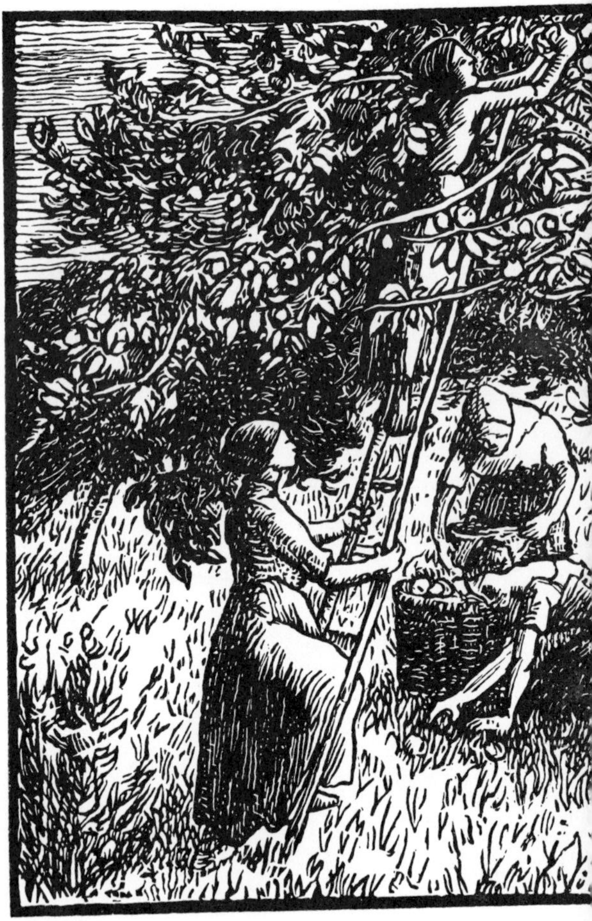

58. Recolte des Pommes after Camille Pissarro (1925)

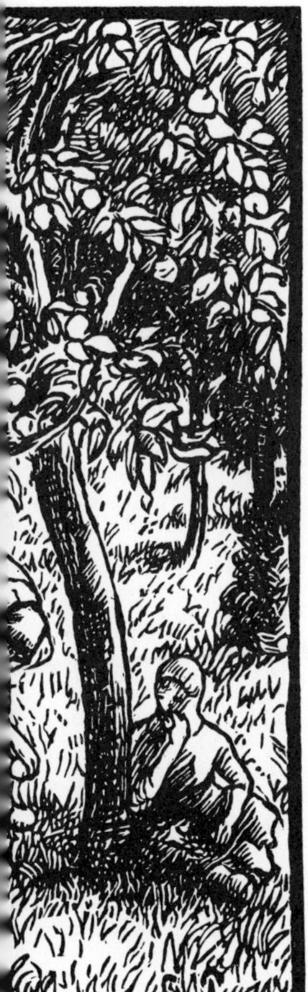

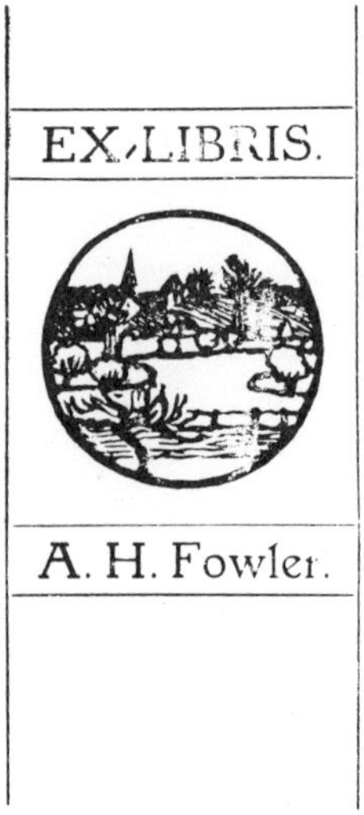

59. Ex libris; *View of Eragnu* (1892); *also A. H.* Fowler *and* in Keats, *La Belle Dame Sans Merci* (1906)

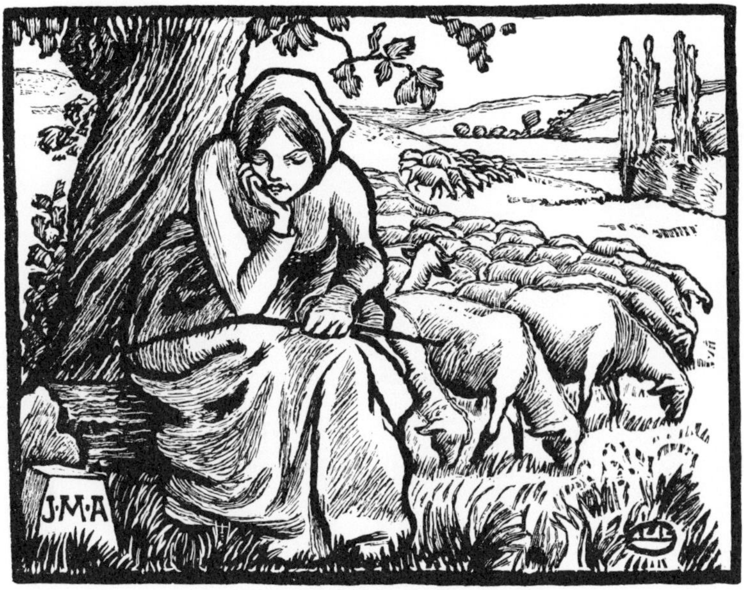

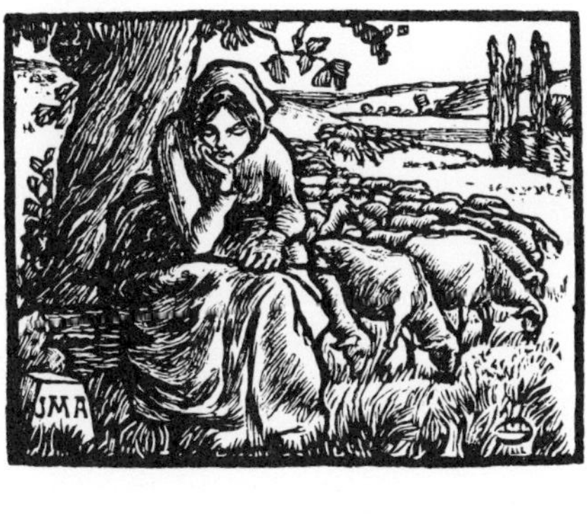

60. Ex libris J. M. Andreini (1907)

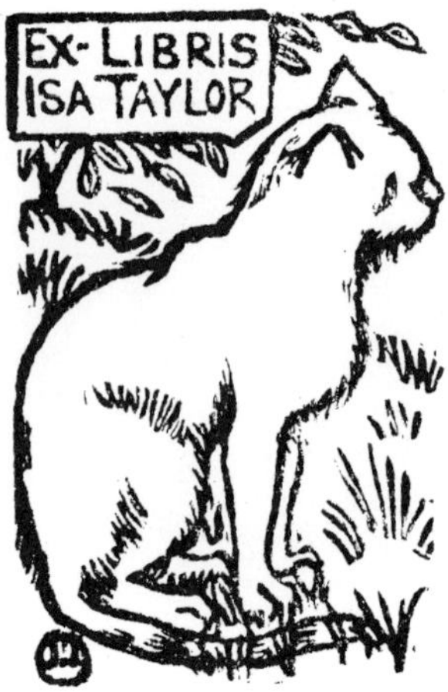

61. Ex libris Isa Taylor, n.d.

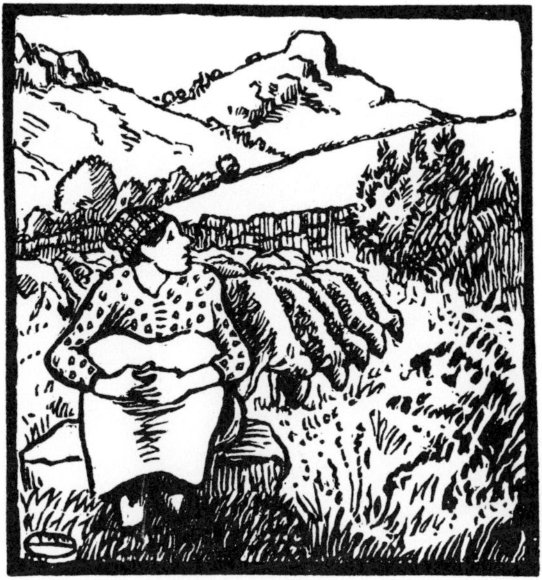

62. La Bergère (1929)

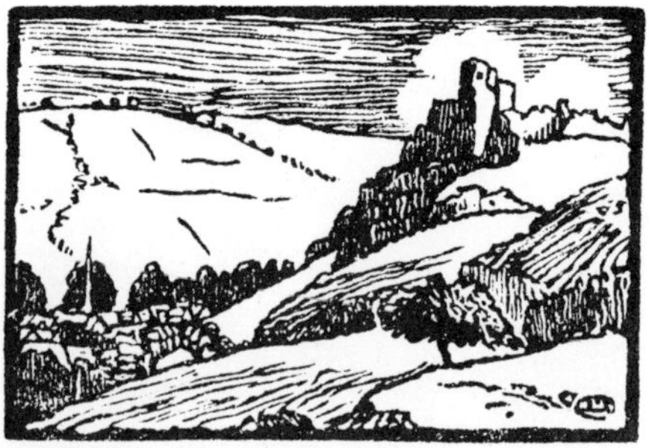

ALL BEST WISHES
FOR THE NEW YEAR
M.CM.XXIV.
FROM
ESTHER, OROVIDA
AND LUCIEN PISSARRO.

The Brook, Stamford Brook,

LONDON.
W. 6.

63. Christmas Card (1924)

MCM.XXV.

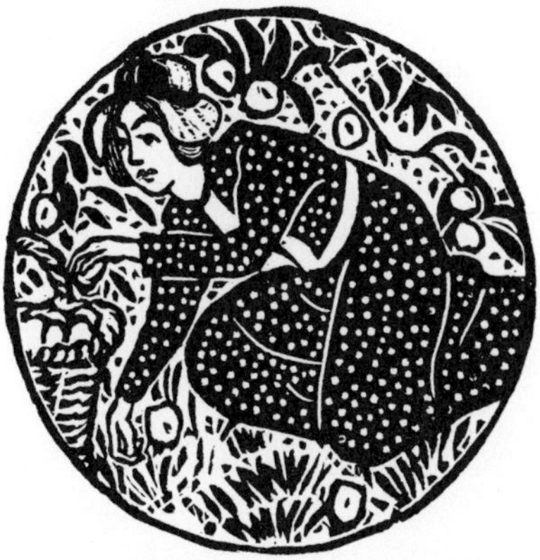

A. ISAACSON SENDS
EVERY GOOD WISH
FOR A HAPPY
XMAS.

9 Aldridge Road Villas. W.11

64. Christmas Card (1925)

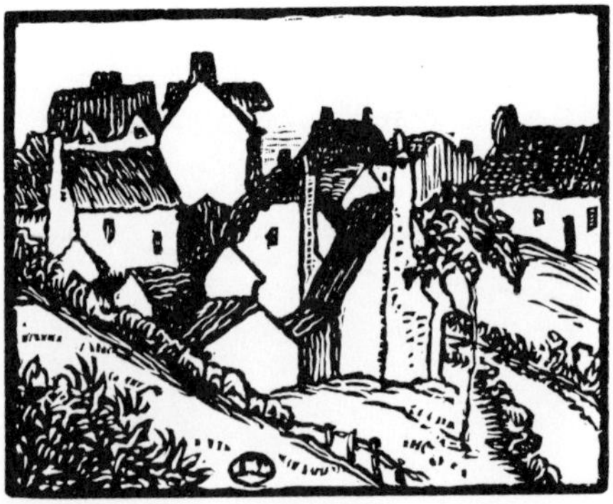

ALL BEST WISHES
FOR THE NEW YEAR
M.CM.XXVII.
FROM
ESTHER, OROVIDA
AND LUCIEN PISSARRO.

The Brook, Stamford Brook,
LONDON.
W. 6.

65. Christmas Card (1927)

CHRONOLOGICAL LIST OF ERAGNY PRESS BOOKS

Rust, Margaret. *The Queen of the Fishes*. London: Eragny Press / Vale Publications, 1894. Edition 150.

Old Testament. *The Book of Ruth and the Book of Esther*. London: Eragny Press / Sold by Hacon and Ricketts, 1896. Edition 155.

Laforgue, Jules (1860-1887). *Moralités Légendaires*, Vol. I. London: Eragny Press / Sold by Hacon and Ricketts, 1897. Edition 220.

Laforgue, Jules (1860-1887). *Moralités Légendaires*, Vol. II. London: Eragny Press / Sold by Hacon and Ricketts, 1898. Edition 220.

Perrault, Charles (1628-1703). *Deux Contes de ma Mere l'Oye - La Belle au Bois Dormant et Le Petit Chaperon Rouge*. London: Eragny Press / Sold by Hacon and Ricketts, 1899. Edition 224.

Flaubert, Gustave (1821-1880). *La Légende de St. Julien l'Hospitalier*. London: Eragny Press / Sold by Hacon and Ricketts, 1900. Edition 226.

Villon, François (b. 1431). *Les Ballades de Maistre François Villon*. London: Eragny Press / Sold by Hacon and Ricketts, 1900. Edition 226.

Flaubert, Gustave (1821-1880). *Un Coeur Simple*. London: Eragny Press / Sold by Hacon and Ricketts, 1901. Edition 226.

Flaubert, Gustave (1821-1880). *Hérodias*. London: Eragny Press / Sold by Hacon and Ricketts, 1901. Edition 226.

Villon, François (b. 1431). *Autres Poesies de Maistre François Villon et Son Ecole*. London: Eragny Press / Sold by Hacon and Ricketts, 1901. Edition 226.

Verhaeren, Emile (1855-1916). *Les Petits Vieux*. London: Eragny Press / Sold by Hacon and Ricketts, 1901. Edition 226.

Bacon, Francis (1561-1626). *Of Gardens. An Essay*. London: Eragny Press/Sold by Hacon and Ricketts,1902. Edition 226.

Ronsard, Pierre de (1524-1585). *Choix de Sonnets.* London: Eragny Press / Sold by Hacon and Ricketts, 1902. Edition 226.

Perrault, Charles (1628-1703). *Histoire de Peau d'Ane.* London: Eragny Press / Sold by Hacon and Ricketts, 1902. Edition 230.

Ronsard, Pierre de (1524-1585). *Abrégé de l'Art Poétique Français.* London: Eragny Press / Sold by Hacon and Ricketts, 1903. Edition 226.

C'est d'Aucassin et de Nicolete. London: Eragny Press / Sold by Hacon and Ricketts, 1903. Edition 230.

Moore, Thomas Sturge (1870-1944). *A Brief Account of the Origin of the Eragny Press and a Note on the Relation of the Printed Book as a Work of Art to Life.* Hammersmith: The Eragny Press, 1903. Edition 241.

White, Diana. *The Descent of Ishtar.* Hammersmith: The Eragny Press, 1903. Edition 226.

Milton, John (1608-1674). *Areopagitica.*1st edition. Hammersmith: The Eragny Press, 1903. Edition 236.

Milton, John (1608-1674). *Areopagitica.* 2nd edition. Hammersmith: The Eragny Press, 1904. Edition 160.

Browning, Robert (1812-1889). *Some Poems by Robert Browning.* Hammersmith: The Eragny Press, 1904. Edition 226.

Coleridge, Samuel Taylor (1772-1834). *Christabel, Kubla Khan, Fancy in Nubibus, and Song from Zapolya.* Hammersmith: The Eragny Press, 1904. Edition 236.

Steele, Robert, editor. *Some Old French and English Ballads.* Hammersmith: The Eragny Press, 1905. Edition 210.

Binyon, Laurence (1869-1943). *Dream Come True.* Hammersmith: The Eragny Press, 1905. Edition 185.

Moore, Thomas Sturge (1870-1944). *The Little School, a Posy of Rhymes.* Hammersmith: The Eragny Press, 1905. Edition 185.

Keats, John (1795-1821). *La Belle Dame sans Merci.* Hammersmith: The Eragny Press, 1906. Edition 210.

Jonson, Ben (1573-1637). *Songs by Ben Jonson. A Selection from the Plays, Masques, and Poems, with the Earliest Known Settings of Certain*

Numbers. Hammersmith: The Eragny Press, 1906. Edition 185.

Rossetti, Christina G. (1830-1894). *Verses by Christina G Rossetti.* Hammersmith: The Eragny Press, 1906. Edition 185.

Perrault, Charles (1628-1703). *Riquet a la Houppe.* Hammersmith: The Eragny Press, 1907. Edition 88.

Nerval, Gérard de (1808-1855). *Histoire de la Reine du Matin et de Soliman Ben Daoud.* Hammersmith: Eragny Press / Paris: Sociètè des Cent Bibliophiles, 1909. Edition 130.

Gautier, Judith (1845-1917). *Poems Tirés du Livre de Jade.* Hammersmith: The Eragny Press, 1911. Edition 130.

Moselly, Emile [pseud. Chénin, Emile] (1870-). *La Charrue d'Erable.* Hammersmith: Eragny Press / Paris: Le Livre Contemporain, 1912. Edition 116.

Field, Michael (Katharine Harris Bradley & Edith Emma Cooper). *Whym Chow: Flame of Love.* Hammersmith: The Eragny Press, 1914. Edition 27.

SELECTED BIBLIOGRAPHY

Arts Council of Great Britain. *Lucien Pissarro 1863 - 1944*. London: Arts Council of Great Britain, 1963.

introduction by Philip James. *Exhibition of Designs and Wood-engravings for the Eragny Press 1894-1914*. London: Arts Council of Great Britain, 1950 (?).

Ashmolean Museum. *Lucien Pissarro: Wood Engravings (29 prints printed from the original blocks now at the Ashmolean)*. Oxford: Ashmolean Museum, 1981.

Bailly-Herzberg, Janine. *Correspondance de Camille Pissarro*. 5 Vols. Presses Universitaires de France, 1980 - 1991.

Bass, Jacquelynn and Field, Richard. *The Artistic Revival of the Woodcut in France 1850 - 1900*. Ann Arbor: Univ. of Michigan Museum of Art, 1984.

Bensusan, Samuel Levy. "The Eragny Press." *Booklover's Magazine*, Edinburgh 8 (1908-09): 119 - 125.

Bensusan-Butt, John. *Recollections of Lucien Pissarro in His Seventies*. London: Anthony d'Offay Gallery, 1977.

The Eragny Press, 1894-1914. Colchester, England: By the Author, 1975.

Bowness, Alan and Laughton, Bruce. *Decade 1890-1900*. Arts Council of Great Britain: Shenval Press, 1967.

Cave, Roderick. *The Private Press*. 2nd ed. New York & London: Bowker & Co., 1983.

Chambers, David. *Lucien Pissarro: Notes on Selection of Wood Blocks Held at the Ashmolean*. Oxford: Ashmolean Museum, 1980.

Clément-Janin. "Lucien Pissarro: Peintres-graveurs contemporains." *Gazette des Beaux-arts*, 15 (1919): 337-51.

Darracott, Joseph. *The World of Charles Ricketts*. London: Cameron and Tayleur, Ltd., 1980.

Fern, Alan, ed. *Lucien Pissarro: Notes on the Eragny Press and Letter to J.B. Manson* (Cambridge Press Book). Cambridge: Cambridge Univ. Press, 1957.

"The Wood-engravings of Lucien Pissarro, with a Catalogue Raisonné." PhD. dissertation, University of Chicago, 1960. 123
Findlay Galleries. *Lucien Pissarro*. New York: Findlay Galleries, 1966.
Franklin, Colin. *The Private Presses*. 2nd ed. England and Vermont: Scolar Press & Gower Publishing Co., 1991.
Garvey, Eleanor M. "Art Nouveau and the French Books of the Eighteen-Nineties." *Harvard Library Bulletin*, XII (1958): 375-391.
Genz, Marcella D. "The History of the Eragny Press 1894-1914." PhD. dissertation, Univ. of Calif., Berkeley, 1990.
Houghton Library, introduction by Peter A. Wick. *The Turn of a Century: Art Nouveau-Jugendstil Books*. Cambridge: Harvard Univ. Dept. of Printing & Graphic Arts, 1970.
Hutton, John. "Les Prolos Vagabondent: Neo-Impressionism and the Anarchist Image of the Trimardeur." *Art Bulletin*, 72 (June 1990): 296-309.
Jackson, Holbrook. *Private Presses in England*. Phila: Lanston Monotype Machine Co., 1923.
Johnson, Una E. *Ambroise Vollard Editeur: 1867-1939. An Appreciation and Catalogue*. New York: Wittenborn and Co., 1944.
Manson, John Bolivar. "Notes on some wood-engravings of Lucien Pissarro." *The Imprint*, London (April 17, 1913): 240-247.
McLean, Ruari. *Modern Book Design from William Morris to the Present Day*. London: Faber & Faber, 1958.
Meadmore, William Sutton. *Lucien Pissarro, Un Coeur Simple*. London, 1962.
Nicolson, Benedict. "The Anarchism of Camille Pissarro." *The Arts*, London, 2 (1947): 43-51.
"Note on Lucien Pissarro." *L'Art Moderne*, Brussels, (6 August 1893).
Perkins, Geoffrey. *The Gentle Art*. Zurich: L'Art Ancien, 1974.
Rewald, John. "Lucien Pissarro. Letters from London, 1883-1891." *Burlington Magazine*, XCI (1949): 188 ff.
editor, with the assistance of Lucien Pissarro. *Camille Pissarro: Letters to His Son Lucien*. New York: Pantheon Books Inc., 1943.

Ricketts, Charles and Pissarro, Lucien. *De la Typographie et de l'Harmonie de la Page Imprimée: William Morris et son influence sur la arts et métiers.* London: Vale Press, 1898.

and Shannon, Charles. *The Dial (an Occasional Publication)* Vols. I - V. London: Ballantyne Press/Hacon and Ricketts,1889-1896.

Robb, Brian. "The Wood-engravings of Lucien Pissarro." *Signature,* n.s. 6 (1948): 36 f.

Roberts, W. "The Print Room, British Museum, Lucien Pissarro." *Magazine of Art,* XXVI (1902): 276-278.

Rose, Jonathan and Anderson, Patricia J., editors. *British Literary Publishing Houses, 1881-1965. Vol. 112: Dictionary of Literary Biography.* Detroit/London: Bruccoli Clark Layman Book, Gale Research Inc., 1991.

Rothenstein, William. *Men and Memories: Recollections of William Rothenstein, 1872-1900.* New York: Coward-McCann, Inc., 1931.

Salaman, Malcolm C. *British Book Illustration Yesterday and To-day.* London: The Studio, Ltd., 1923.

Stetz, Margaret D. and Lasner, Mark Samuels. *England in the 1890s: Literary Publishing at the Bodley Head.* Washington, D.C.: Georgetown University Press, 1990.

Symons, Arthur J.A. "An Unacknowledged Movement in Fine Printing, the Typography of the Eighteen-Nineties." *The Fleuron,* VII (1930): 83-119.

Taylor, John Russell. *The Art Nouveau Book in Britain.* Cambridge, MA: MIT Press , 1966.

Thorold, Anne. "The Pissarro Collection in the Ashmolean Museum, Oxford." *Burlington Magazine,* (October 1978).

Catalogue of Oil Paintings of Lucien Pissarro. London: Athelney Books, 1983.

ed. *Letters of Lucien to Camille Pissarro, 1883-1903.* Volume in Cambridge Studies in the History of Art. Cambridge: Cambridge University Press, 1993.

Pissarro: Monde Rural - Art - Politique. Exhibition Catalogue: Centre Culturel du Marais, 4 fev - 26 avril, 1981.

Vollard, Ambroise. *Recollections of a Picture Dealer.* New York: Dover Publications, Inc., 1978.

PISSARRO
E·ET·L·
LONDON.
ERAGNY PRESS

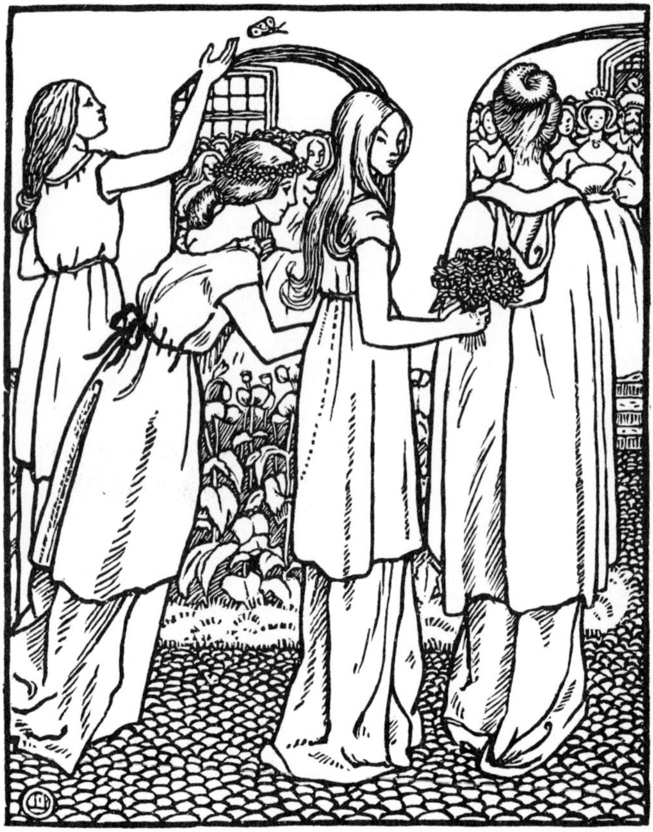

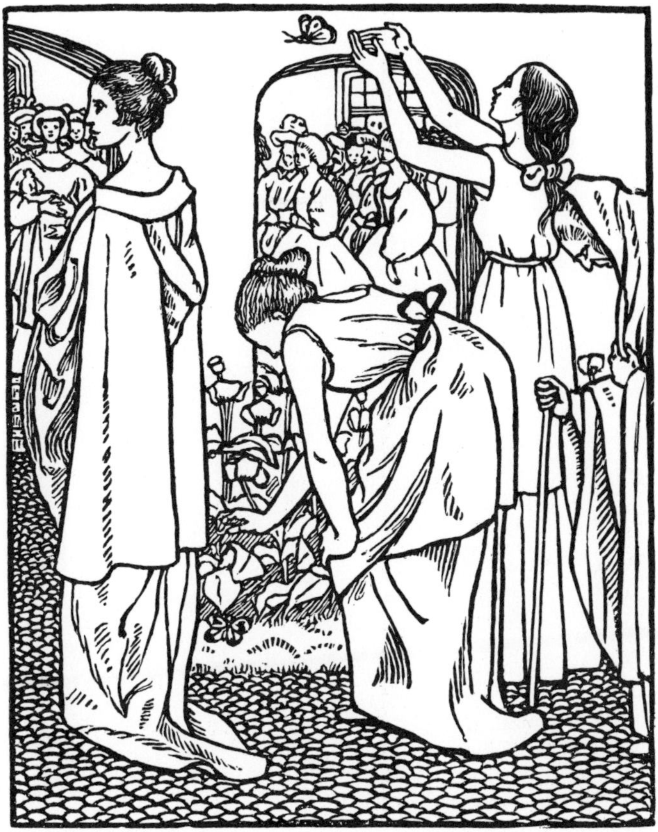